DEDICATION

We dedicate this book to each person who really wants to be successful. It is possible with precision, dedicated effort, and good works.

To the people in my life who have been generous with their time, support, and guidance on my journey to success. To those who are just starting their journey, know that you are not alone.

To my wonderful husband Steve, for his unconditional love and support…it has meant so much to me. To my two sons, Max and Travis Eisenberg and my new daughter-in law, Jamie. To my parents, James and Virginia Waters and my sisters Karen Pine and Lora Gwinn. And to my new grandson, Owen James Eisenberg, who will make me a proud grandma.

Donna

To women in business for untold amounts of endurance, creativity, and courage—please know that YOU are the gift.

For treasured memories and everlasting legacies, I remain grateful to you—Aunt Jerry Eileen Perry, Reverend Delores Francine McMillan, Good Friend Allison Fisher, and Grandmother Dorothy Bernice Johnson.

Thank You, God. May each person touched by these works receive some of Your preciousness as a result.

Jo Lena

Commit to the Lord, whatever you do,
and your plans will succeed.
Proverbs 16:3 (NIV)

If You

Really

Want to Be Successful,

Get
Connected!

Wisdom, Insights, and Strategies
from Entrepreneurial Women

by

Jo Lena Johnson and
Donna Gamache

MISSION POSSIBLE PRESS
Creating Legacies through Absolute Good Works
www.jolenajohnson.com
www.GetConnectedBook.com

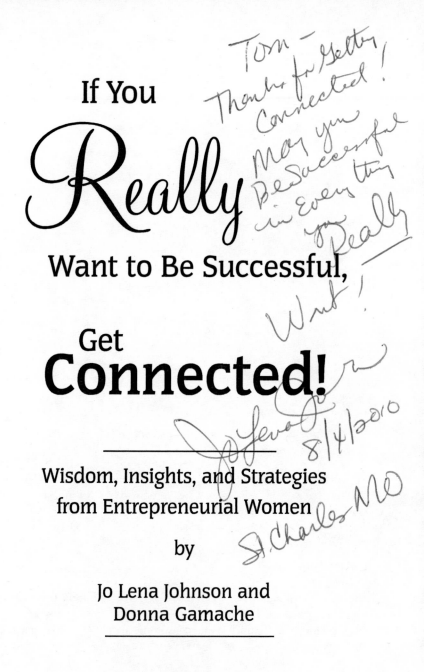

Handwritten inscription: Tom — Thanks for Getting Connected! May you Be Successful in Everything you Really Want! Jo Lena Jo 8/4/2010 St. Charles MO

The Mission is Possible.
Sharing love and wisdom for the young and "the young at heart,"
expanding minds,
restoring kindness through
good thoughts, feelings, and attitudes
is our intent.
May you thrive and be good in all you are and all you do…
Be Cause U.R. Absolute Good!

Scripture quotations are from *The Holy Bible, The New Open Bible Study Edition (KJV)* © 1990 by Thomas Nelson, Inc. Other scriptural references are from Biblegateway.com (NIV).

If You Really Want to Be Successful, Get Connected! Wisdom, Insights, and Strategies from Entrepreneurial Women

ISBN 978-0-9827520-2-9

The intent of the authors and publisher is only to offer information to help you in your journey. In the event that you use any of the information in this book for yourself, which is your constitutional right, the author and the publisher assume no responsibility for your actions.

Published by Mission Possible Press. Logos and marks are trademarks of the publisher. For information, contact Absolute Good Training and Life Skills Management at training@absolutegood.com.

Our Mission: Putting Good in the Universe

Donna Gamache has a lot to share—and I believe you will be enriched by her wisdom and experiences. She is committed to service and to connecting people to their true passions and success. When producing this work I have been delighted, enlightened, and inspired by her. Donna has shared information I didn't know, insights I hadn't considered, and wisdom that I really want everyone to know.

Donna and I have both had several successful businesses, made lots of mistakes, and gone into utter poverty at the expense of our "business ventures." Our intent is to give you some things to consider; being a business owner is not easy, especially if you are trying to run a successful business in a principled or spiritually grounded way. Honestly, business ownership is not for everyone. May you find these pages to be helpful on your quest to become a new, established, or former business owner.

The opportunity which Donna and I are afforded is to help people be prepared for success. Throughout the book, you will hear directly from Donna, in her own words—as she told them to me during our interviews. We also switch formats—and I include the questions I asked, her answers, and, at times, my commentary.

We promise to be open, forthcoming, and true to you—based on our own experiences, with input from some of our wise friends, mentors, and other women business owners. Donna and I appreciate the opportunity and privilege to share with you—and to add to your life through our connected purposes on this earth…

Jo Lena Johnson, Creator
"If You Really Want to…" book series

FOREWORD

I have always been an advocate for women, wanting to help each be successful as they work in and on their businesses. One thing I know for sure is that no one makes it alone. It takes more than passion and dedication to start, grow, and to scale a business. It takes "access" to information, tools, resources, relationships, and leads! This book will give you access to women from all over the United States who willingly share stories of struggle and triumph as they have built their own businesses. I highly recommend and encourage you to read what other women entrepreneurs share about their journeys to success.

As you read, you'll gain access to the wisdom these entrepreneurial women share. You'll gain powerful insights from them on how to establish a good name, build relationships, honor yourself and others, brand your enterprise, and much more. Without question, through their commitment to help *"lift as they climb,"* you will benefit abundantly as over 20 successful businesswomen share their personal strategies on everything from the power of vision to the criticality of excellent customer service.

Jo Lena Johnson and Donna Gamache have done an outstanding job of answering questions and addressing key issues that women in business commonly face. With professionalism, compassion, and experienced wisdom, this book will support any person in business in making better decisions, gaining confidence, understanding the fundamentals of developing strategic relationships, creating a solid business model, building an efficient infrastructure, and monetizing your dreams!

Sandra Yancey
Founder and CEO
eWomenNetwork, Inc.

Share with US

We would be honored to hear your thoughts and activities in response to this book. Let us know what your favorite portions are and how they affect you or your life, by emailing getconnected@absolutegood.com.

Meet US

We invite you to share your projects and efforts to "put good in the Universe," whether the efforts are personal stories from home, large-scale projects in your community, or a force that has beamed around the globe.

We teach, we speak, and we travel to connect with people—conducting training sessions, workshops, and classes to help tell stories, build legacies, and to learn more ways to focus on the purpose and success of others.

Contribute Good, Too

This book is the second of four books in the "*If You Really Want to…*" series. With each book, at least 20% of sales go toward putting more good in the universe by supporting tangible projects and generating good work. Working together, we can create more resources, more wisdom, more access, and support more young people. Creating good together helps everyone.

Contact Us Today. Email at:
Goodworks@absolutegood.com
or visit www.jolenajohnson.com.

Table of Contents

SECTION THREE

THE ACCELERATION ~ CONNECTING AND RELATING

SECTION FOUR
THE TOOLS ~ RESOURCES AND TIPS

SECTION FIVE
THE REARVIEW MIRROR ~ REFLECTIONS

Section One
The Scenic Route

There's No Easy
Road to Success

Do You Know What You *Really* Want?

Jo Lena Johnson

*"If you don't know where you want to go,
a map won't help you."*

In order to be successful, just knowing something is not enough. Practice and experience make "skilled." Getting wisdom and understanding, along with discernment, are crucial. I urge you to have an attitude of achievement, along with guided, orderly steps, and to get a plan of action. This means calling on your resources; it could be through a business coach, through prayer, or through getting a mentor—conceptualizing simply isn't enough. Getting connected with knowledge and wisdom is what is needed for you to be successful.

Starting with questions is a really good way to begin and to clarify your journey. It's not enough to say, "I'm going there" or "this is my goal." You must also know where you are, know where you intend to go, possess the tools, become skilled at using them, and know how to get there. By connecting with those who have achieved success in your area of interest, you save valuable time and precious energy, considering questions and contemplating the answers given.

We all have factors which interrupt our success.

It's Your Choice! Choose a Destination and Thrive!

What do you really want? So many times people focus on what they don't want in life and forget about what they do want. Of course, in making a big purchase decision such as a car, a home, or other real estate, we tend to take our time and do the research. We do so because we know a significant amount of money is on the line.

However, step back and think about other important areas of your life—your day-to-day thoughts, feelings, habits, and practices.

Are you satisfied and joyful, worried and afraid, or concerned and encouraged? Whatever your current state, your thoughts will dictate your new results or keep you in the comfort or discomfort zone of whatever is normal for you.

When you secure a new contract or receive an unexpected check in the mail, it's easy to "claim" what we did well, and share the news with the right people. However, saying, "I underbid on a contract, and don't know how I'm going to fulfill my commitment," may not be as easy to express. Negative things are difficult to acknowledge to ourselves, let alone to tell others.

Your daily activities have the most impact on you, your family, and others who are in your life. My mentor, the late Reverend Delores McMillan, would say to me, "Whatever you think about, you bring about." Depending on what topic we were discussing at the time, I had to really consider what I had done to cause the situation, circumstance, or challenge.

Another of Rev. McMillan's favorite sayings to me was "Leave it alone; leave it all the way alone!" She would usually tell me this when we were discussing possible partnerships in business (I was working in Hollywood at the time) or in the area of relationships. I am grateful that our relationship was one of trust, mutual love, and respect because through mistakes and successes, she made it safe enough to share.

It's good to have people in your life that care enough to recognize who you are, love you in spite of yourself, and who support you through your challenges or blind spots.

There are actually a lot of brilliant people in this world, including you. Yet if you don't make time to appreciate yourself, your priorities, and your effect on others, you may miss the opportunity to connect to the success you desire and deserve.

Do you realize that you draw people to you every day?

You might have heard of "the law of attraction" or other similar principles found in books like the best-seller "The Secret." Your life, world, and affairs are what you make them. You model for yourself and others—and with clear vision, steadfast tenacity, resourcefulness, guidance, and a foundation based on solid principles—you can have what you *really* want if you are willing to do the work.

Now, let's talk about other things that matter—relationships, communication, and personal responsibility. It's all about choosing healthy habits, routinely. Enjoy the people with and for whom you spend the most time loving, supporting, and providing. I urge you to look forward to opportunities to grow, expand, and to make new choices that will impact your life positively, if you chose to consider them.

When you know what you *really* want, are willing to search for input from experts, and take action, you can and will achieve your goals. One of the biggest challenges, though, is when goals are not financial or tangible—when they are about those we love, quality of relationships, personal peace, satisfaction, and self-care...you know...work-life balance.

Days can be spent focused on earning money, saving money, investing money, and spending money. They can be filled with meetings, schedules, routines, daily responsibilities, and old habits that die hard.

In order to gain greater understanding, it takes clarity of purpose, flexibility, willingness, making good choices, and overcoming obstacles.

Getting a mentor helps. As we move forward, you will meet women who share with you from experience—from our heads and our hearts. As you read what we share, begin to examine how you can apply the lessons, the information, and the recommendations to your particular situation and business. Applying sound wisdom can save you time, money, and perhaps heartbreak!

For example, you'll meet Angel Were, who knew during college that she wanted to make a difference. Now, she is fairly new to "entrepreneurialism" and wants to take her business to the next level. She does not have all of the answers—and recognizes it. What a glorious place to be! Angel was kind enough to ask the questions which many would-be successful people should ask and often don't. You can learn from this.

Being a mentor helps too. On the other side, each of us possesses unique experience that, if shared openly, could help others avoid some costly mistakes or choices. Yet, in my experience, many are not forthcoming in sharing those things when it could make a real difference for another.

You'll also meet Tessa Greenspan, an experienced business woman who, after selling her multi-million dollar grocery business, continues to give, share, and mentor through her new health venture and through her words, kind ways, and heart. You can learn directly from this.

Recognizing the need is your choice! If you notice that someone is in need of help, especially when they may not recognize it, step in and help out. If you notice that you are not getting the results you really want, connect in (to self), and then reach out. Thriving is a really good destination.

Connecting Starts with You!

"Examine yourselves…"
2 Corinthians 13:5

Relating to people starts with willingness to share

Have you been in need of some information, resource, or guidance and you just kept it to yourself? Have you heard of the saying "a closed mouth never gets fed?" At this time in society, technology has given us the ability to "go global" and to "connect" with people who would not otherwise know we exist, yet advancement is coming at a cost. As people focus on self-promotion and the accolades of their products or services, we have been losing civility and caring. Understanding who you are, your purpose, and why you would choose a career, an occupation, a job, or your own business means investing in your future.

So, are you a business owner or an entrepreneur? There are differences. It's important to know who you are so that you can clearly define your goals!

Entrepreneur: Someone who assumes the financial risk of the initiation, operation, and management of a business. *(Definition from Entrepreneur magazine)*

Are you most interested in innovation and driven by the desire to change things, situations, or circumstances?

Alternatively, are you steady and pretty comfortable with established business models and traditional methods of goal setting and compensation?

A small business owner may choose to establish a franchise of an existing business with a pre-formulated model for conducting business. This could include direct marketing companies or industrial cleaning companies.

Depending on the industry, the initial investment will vary from extremely nominal (less than $100 to join and begin as a distributor, for example), or could be costly, some franchises require more than $200,000 to open the doors.

Do you know about the E-Myth?

The 'Entrepreneurial Myth' or E-Myth is the mythic assumption is that an expert in a given technical field will also be expert at running that kind of business. Additional business management skills are needed to keep a business running smoothly. *(Definition from Wikipedia.org)*

These questions may seem insignificant, yet the answers speak to the heart of your true desires, and will assist you in making informed and wise choices about your endeavors.

We devoted an entire "Small Business Considerations" section from Wikipedia in the resources section of this book which will support you in making choices for how you will create success after you have considered what we share.

For now, please begin to identify your true passions and modern realities of your particular situation.

Once you have "connected" with yourself, your level of comfort with risk and reward, your vision, and goals for the future, you are in a better position to relate and to share with others.

Unemployed or Self-Employed?

"Honey, you've always wanted to be in business and now you are!"

Wisdom from Canadian Business Woman Anne Boody

The day after I was let go, I was feeling relieved, yet numb because I had always received accolades for my work. I decided to go out to walk my dog and walk off some fear and anger. En route, I ran into a neighbor who asked how I was doing. I didn't know her well, yet I answered openly and I told her that I had been let go from my job just the day before. "You may not believe it now but it was probably the best thing that could have happened," she said. She then shared that she too had "workplace issues" a few years back. She gave me the positive input I needed at that very moment, which was a re-affirmation that the circumstances could be a blessing in disguise. Out of that conversation, a friendship blossomed and we have continued to support each other since, over ten years ago.

When I returned from that walk, my husband said, "Honey, you've always wanted to be in business and now you are!" He had set up my makeshift "desk" on a banquet table he had dragged into the living room. And that was that. The paper was stacked, the Day-Timer was open, and the phone was there, just waiting for me to start marketing myself.

Battling fear, keeping tears back, with a tremendous sense of relief, I was about to see what was on the horizon. That was 11 years ago. I don't believe in coincidences; I believe in God instances. My first major contract was just around the corner. It was through a two-part equation, connection and merit that one contract led to another.

Connection (Networking + Rapport) and Merit ("Attitude Abilities" + "Capabilities") equals success. You have to believe that you are doing the absolute best you can—and not just riding on someone else's coat tails. Because of the values and capabilities I brought, before I knew it, I had major contracts coming from people I had worked with in the past and everything just fell into place.

That enabled me to have the resources to commence a wrongful dismissal case. I didn't dwell on it and I wasn't starved out—I continued with the legal challenge—and with my life. Sometimes what seems like the bleakest situation is a blessing in disguise.

Who would have ever thunk it? I would end up traveling across Canada, meeting so many different people, and dealing with a diversity of issues—and I gained the flexibility I was looking for in my life. I just wouldn't have had the life I have had over the past decade if it had not happened.

Jo Lena: Please explain a little about what you actually do, and what you are up to these days.

Anne: I provide communications advice through my consultancy—including marketing and communications planning; strategic positioning for products or policy placements; and writing of all sorts—speech writing, website writing. My dream would be to write a speech for President Barack Obama.

Jo Lena: I'm surprised to hear that, since you are Canadian. Why would you want to write a speech for our United States president?

Anne: I find him an inspiration—a person who has been able to bridge gaps; he has a vision, a purpose, and a sense of humility, and those are attributes I find refreshing. It doesn't matter the nationality, it's what he embodies: the value system and principles that attract me. He speaks with compassion and sincerity. What better person can you write for than somebody like that? He's true leadership as far as I'm concerned and there is a lot of that lacking in this world.

Jo Lena: I know you really mean that. Your passion and way with words continues to warm my heart! I'm not sure how many Canadians are on his team. However, knowing your abilities, I'm sure he'd do well to give you an opportunity to craft a speech. What's next for you?

Anne: I'm building my client base to weather the economic challenges. It's put a dent in the business, yet, rather than being gripped by fear, I work on taking an action step every single day.

Jo Lena: What do you do to handle it?

Anne: It starts with being grateful for what I do have and then it continues through the day with positive affirmations, networking, and using the downtime productively. It's amazing how many people I've linked up with—some I've spoken with are people from 20 or 30 years ago! I try to focus and work on my guiding view; none of us knows what's around the corner. Rather than fear it, dare to take the path! I take the position that life is one heck of an adventure that will bring untold opportunities. I suggest that people look at life as an adventure rather than something to be feared.

I can get myself into a tizzy sometimes, and let fear creep in—that's when you have to step back and practice faith. I have to really exercise the spiritual dimension of my life—that's what I continue to work at.

To be quite honest, it's easier to say than do but, if you just keep telling yourself, you'll start to believe it. That's where faith comes in. Believing that you are where you are meant to be, and that things happen for a reason. However, individual choice comes into the picture as well. We can each choose to live in the fear of uncertainty or choose to take the right action that would take you (us) into the new opportunity.

It's flipping the coin, in my view—choosing to exist in the negative or grow in the positive.

Get Connected with Anne through
Spearhead Communications and Marketing Inc.
at anneboody@rogers.com

Invest Your Passion for Long-Term Success

*"Being a real estate agent may not be what you want to
do if you simply like to look at houses or curtains."*

Wisdom from Karen Schindler

Once you've mastered the day-to-day tasks, it's important to "check
in" and assess if what you are up to is going to provide you long-
term success. Passion is typically a prerequisite for sustaining your
business.

Karen shared her personal story as well as helpful things to consider
when thinking about "self-employment," as she calls it. She also offers
insight into the power of business referrals. We learned from Karen
that her success has taken courage, support, planning, and heart.

Why did you choose real estate?

I didn't plan it. I went into a business school program after high
school and they offered job placement. I secured a job in residential
(apartment) property management, and I got a real estate license at
that time. I really enjoyed helping people find the apartment they
were looking for. But I was limited to that complex, and I wasn't paid
very well. So went away to college, got my degree, and thought I was
going to get a job. It's one of the great myths—get out of school and
start earning $30,000 or $40,000—well, that's not how it turned
out.

During my job search I got into commercial property management. It wasn't as rewarding as residential property management. Where people place a desk doesn't excite people as much as where they will raise their kids, so I was working and not really fulfilled. I spoke with Sandy, a family friend, who had left a "good corporate job" in order to sell real estate. I told her I wanted to sell houses for a living and wanted to know what I could do over the next year to "get" prepared to quit my job and go into real estate successfully.

I ended up having an interview with her. She talked with me some in her office and I went on some appointments with her. She asked me if I would be interested in working with her as a buyer specialist because she had more work than she could handle and I said no. I was 23 and didn't have much money in savings; I was living check to check, and couldn't imagine taking a job where I didn't have guaranteed income. She still encouraged me to work with her, and after I shadowed her for 4 weeks, she helped me to put together a strategy that made sense to me.

She asked questions like, "What are you making now?" and "What are your bills?" Then she shared crucial information like "A realistic sales amount would be $xxx; plus income would be $xxx." I knew the work was more satisfying than my "job" and it seemed safer because I would be working with an established team that they had built up. Yet, if I was going to be successful, I needed to invest as well.

Some of the initial business expenses included:

1. Buying another car because my college car wasn't appropriate for client showings.

2. Paying for my own health insurance because I was self-employed and had no benefits.

3.   Local and national association dues and a "key" for opening lock boxes.

I considered these expenses and the risk I would be taking, and I figured that with a strong foundation, continued support, and my passion for the work, I would net more money than my "salary." So I let go of fear and tried it. That was 13 years ago and I have been in residential real estate the whole time.

Four Things I Really Want You Know About Being Self-Employed:

1.   **Being self-employed definitely has some great advantages.** You control your own destiny—there is no ceiling to what you can achieve and there is no guarantee you will achieve anything.

2.   **There are disadvantages.** You put in a lot of work on the front end. However, the rewards come in the back end. In real estate, you start back at zero every year, and if you don't sell anything this month, it doesn't matter what you sold last year, the year before, or the month before.

3.   **Real estate may not be what you want to do if you simply like to look at houses, or just want creative inspiration.** At least once a month somebody says, "It would be so fun to see all those curtain decorating ideas." Knock on your neighbor's doors all day and get excited that way!

4.   **It's never just about a house—it is social work more than sales work.** Reasons people sell include: "We've had another child so we need another home," "Mom's passed away and have to sell her home," or "We're getting married and we

need to sell two houses and buy a third one." It's usually about a transition of some kind, which may be a happy occasion, or it may be a stressful life occurrence.

Things I've Learned Through My Business About Human Nature:

Selling a home is disruptive to people's routines—people get out of their comfort zones. To buy a house typically is fun. To sell a house is more stressful; it's easier to buy, especially if it's your first house because it's not personal to you.

However, when selling it *is* personal for you. Hearing people make statements about your home, things they don't like, or being told reasons it's not right, is stressful. Being aware of people's circumstances, needs, desires, and goals is crucial. I comfort people through it while fulfilling the ethical duties of my license and life's work.

Three Keys to Karen's Success:

I like to surround myself with positive quotes and positive energy.

1. I focus on what I'm grateful for—what I focus on or what goes right expands.

2. To be where I am—if I'm at home with my daughter, I don't let other people interrupt. I try to stay focused on that activity at that time, when I'm doing it.

3. I do what I say I'm going to do—and I am on time.

Business Networking International (BNI), Building Relationships, and Referrals

In addition to running her successful real estate business, Karen also serves as the vice president of the "St. Louis Success Net" BNI Chapter. **BNI** is the largest *business networking* organization in the world. They offer members the opportunity to share ideas, contacts, and most important, *business referrals*. She's been in the organization almost two years and shares how connecting through the organization has been beneficial.

Karen Shares Benefits of Membership in BNI:

1. Professionally, BNI has allowed me to build relationships with other small business owners to share success and to solve challenges. Training, hiring, and challenges: these are things we all have had to deal with and we can learn from each other on what works and what hasn't worked.

2. I've made some good friends, people I would not have had a chance to know; and to be around other successful people. My business has increased—after 13 years and being established—BNI has represented about 20% of the business I've had over the last year.

3. I have an extended sales force. When I run into people who need insurance, I refer them to Glenn Eckert, who has been in insurance for over 27 years. With the economy, I meet people who might have been laid off and have a 401k to roll over so, I can refer them to Jeff Rogles, who is a whiz at financial planning solutions. They do the same for me.

Organizations like BNI are successful because they accept members who are established business owners with proven records of accomplishment who are committed to growing and building their enterprises. They are a tremendously influential group, with chapters throughout the United States and many countries. If you are serious about growing through connections, it will require approval for membership, and a commitment to attend weekly meetings. Everyone should know how it works—and BNI has an outstanding model that really works.

Learn more about BNI by going to www.bni.com.
Get connected to Karen at
www.KarenSchindlerTeam.com—
just tell her Jo Lena and Donna referred you!

From Nursing to Jewelry, a Sparkling Journey

"She was making $10,000 a month in this business and I thought that if Jennifer could do it, I could do it."

Wisdom from Marty Hoerman

Marty Hoerman spent over 25 years as a nurse before rising to the level of division manager for lia sophia, a fashion jewelry company which has direct sales advisors and who primarily do home parties to sell their jewelry. She's been with the company for 4 years, and her position is third level in the company's multi-level marketing plan.

Marty is warm, welcoming, and a great communicator. She attributes a great amount of her success to the people skills she gained in nursing. Marty's is a story of a woman, helper, and business professional who was inspired.

How did you come to work with lia sophia?

My daughter-in-law, Julie, had a lia sophia party and her friend, Jennifer was the Advisor. Jennifer shared the story of her mother's success and her own story of success. At the time, Jennifer was making $10,000 a month in this business after only 18 months. So I thought that if Jennifer could do it, I could do it, too. I did my research on the company and everything that I read was positive—and seemed to be everything I was looking for.

I wanted to be around women—I needed more social time—I needed a change. The opportunity seemed to be everything I was looking for. I hadn't really ever bought much jewelry. I'm a pretty conservative farm girl from Kansas and I hadn't really spent much money on myself. I also liked the idea of the challenge to start my own business.

So, having the opportunity to have some jewelry was interesting, and the money was why we do business. And, because my husband had been in sales, I knew sales could be lucrative. With my communication skills as a nurse, I figured I could help people get started in this business and help them reach their goals also.

When you are a nurse, you come into contact with a very wide selection of people who communicate in different ways. I learned how to communicate toward a person's needs and interests. So when I meet people, I have been able to speak with them about this business and how it could fit into their particular situation and meet their needs.

That enabled me to identify with a wide variety of partners that work with me in this business. We can work together and figure out how to best support each person in the way they need. We work together and bounce ideas off each other. It also helps because my strengths may be different from someone else's. In actuality, we share each of our strengths, and each of our businesses grows stronger because of it.

Our Tag Line is *"Share the Love of Jewelry"*

To become successful with lia sophia we make it duplicatable. We share with our new partners everything that we do—from getting ready for a show to booking parties. We share what works, and what doesn't work. Some people can pick up things they are more comfortable doing, based on their personality and creativity. We don't make it complicated—we share our ideas, documents, flyers, and everything. We want our partners to be successful because in reality, if they are successful, we are successful.

"If they are successful, we are successful." What does that really mean?

When I was a nurse, I helped others. I feel like I am helping people more now than I did as a nurse because they are growing, bringing in money for their families, and building a new career—just like I have.

This business is so easy. When we can find someone who wants to try, it's very lucrative, very part time, and on the side—anyone can learn to do it.

What we do find is that those who stick with it and are self-starters will be successful.

Those who aren't self-starters will fall off. We are looking for people who want to build the business and see the big picture.

You used the term partners several times, is that an official term or a state of mind?

They are team members or associates—we just help each other—when we do a training or opportunity event, we can pull on each other's strengths and it's kind of fun learning who can do what, so it feels like a partnership, and in essence, it is.

What are reasons a woman should consider going into this type of "self-employment" business?"

1. Mentors are available to answer questions.

2. The investment is minimal, and they can stop at any time.

3. The personal and professional development opportunity builds confidence and skills. We grow slowly into where we are at the time—I never thought of myself as a leader or a manager. Just like many, I was scared of presenting, and worked through that; then I got more comfortable talking with people about the opportunity. We each continue to grow, so personal growth just happens.

4. With the economy, our jewelry has been sort of recession-proof. It is affordable, sells itself, and while women aren't buying as many "big ticket" items, they still want to do something for themselves. We have a variety of different styles suited for everyone. Our price point is key, our quality is guaranteed, and our jewelry is for the masses. There's something for everyone and we see women evolve.

What Are Four Things That You Do Every Day For Yourself And For Your Success?

1. I answer my emails and I answer my phone; I communicate with them. When they need something, they can count on me. I communicate with my family, my team, and my friends. I think communication is huge with success.

2. I'm a real task person—so I make sure that my work gets done before I play. My mom taught me that a long time ago. I do the actual work first and when I need to get on the phone, I call people, finding shows and following up with leads. Calls are huge in this business.

3. I read the Bible regularly and pray a lot. We all need to know that there is someone out there who is watching over us, and that there is hope that our prayers are answered.

4. I pray about my business too—I have to have some trust and some hope that this will continue—and having my faith, and God as my true mentor, I can have the confidence in moving forward in each new day that has me connect with more people.

Any final thoughts?

Always look at your business as you are helping others—sharing with other women who want to make a difference in their lives.

Some of my very best friends and family are in this business with me—I've made many very good friends. It has accomplished what I was looking for: social outings, meeting new people, the challenge of running my own business, and financial success. Everyone deserves these things, especially when they really want them and put out the effort to obtain them.

Get Connected with Marty at
martyhoerman@charter.net
or at www.liasophia.com/martyhoerman.

Four Steps to Vision and Success

"You must continually pursue your vision, your dreams; and you must stay abreast of changes."

Wisdom from Dr. Candace T. Wakefield

1. **Believe in God.** He knows what's in your future; put your trust and faith in Him, and let Him guide you. Never let someone tell you what you can't do. I ran into that with counselors and deans in my career. Never let someone talk you out of your own potential.

2. **Always invest in your education.** It's what will take care of you, and it will pay for itself in the end. Don't be afraid to pursue it because of costs. The value will be well worth it.

3. **If there is something you really believe in, stick with it.** There was no Plan B for me when I was pursuing my dream. The pursuit meant that I was going forward, regardless.

Even when it gets hard and difficult, and dentistry is not for the faint of heart, things are going to happen. Then you have to step up your game and improve. You can't float and let things pass by. You must continually pursue your vision, your dreams, and you must stay abreast of changes. Technology does not stop once you get out of school.

4. **If you want to build the best business, you have to compete to become the best.** Constantly prepare yourself. Education is always changing, like sports and technology.

Creating the "Children's Dental Zone"

Dr. Wakefield spent 4 years working in a research lab while gaining her BA in Biological Sciences at the University of Missouri-Columbia. She then attended Southern Illinois University School of Dental Medicine and graduated in May 2000 with a D.M.D. (Doctor of Dental Medicine). Dr. Wakefield was prepared, motivated, and educated, ready to succeed in her dental practice. She didn't stop there! She obtained a Certificate in Pediatric Dentistry in May 2002 from Howard University.

In September 2005 she became board certified in Pediatric Dentistry. This was an optional certification (in dentistry); it's the icing on the cake. At the time of her receiving the certification, she was the only female board certified pediatric dentist in the state of Missouri.

A dentist named "Candy," Dr. Wakefield is also a vibrant presenter and speaks to audiences about success strategies, vision, and work ethic. This soon-to-be author is also completing a children's book about the "stress-free fun times" to be had at the dentist's office.

Meet "Dr. Candy" at www.thechildrensdentalzone.com
or www.facebook/thechildrensdentalzone.com.

Having it All

*"Truly charity has no limit...bloom in the
garden where He has planted..."*
St. Francis de Sales

Wisdom from Deborah Shorter

Deborah Shorter has been the wife of Vincent Shorter for 19
years. They have three children, Courtney, and twins Ashley and
Christopher. Her life as a military wife showed her how to build
skills, build a business, and maintain a household while her husband
was serving our country.

Her background is public/media relations. She is currently manager
of Global Accounts for HelmsBriscoe as an independent consultant
who now has the flexibility to plan her own travel schedule, as well
as meeting the planning needs of her global client base.

As women in business, it's often difficult to balance our relationship
status with our aspirations for professional success.

Deborah explains that being a military wife was challenging—filling
in the gaps and handling things that her husband would do when
he was with the family. Be you single, in partnership, married, or
desiring to be any of the previous, appreciating, and caring for self,
family, and business interests can be challenging to even the most
creative and resourceful person. Through briefly sharing her story,

Deborah shows us how to overcome challenges and to be successful by being connected with what you *really* want.

Deborah Shorter Shares Her Top Five Skills

1. Multi-tasking and managing several projects at one time
2. I'm creative—often finding new ways to do things
3. I'm organized
4. My ability to lead a project and see it to the end
5. I'm a problem solver—positively affecting a situation—and I know how to discern, pick, and choose my battles

Though my husband is now retired, I've been married half of my life. At such a young age, I chose to find creative ways to fulfill my responsibilities and to maintain my identity.

Five Challenges to Managing Military Family Life

1. Keeping myself as an important piece in the puzzle— it's easy to lose yourself in raising the kids and being a wife of a military officer when the nation's mission is first priority.
2. Being able to continue with my own life goals.
3. Keeping lasting friendships, through our various moves and stages of life.
4. Being married and managing being a "single parent," when duty calls.
5. Helping family and friends to understand the differences of priorities, focus, and responsibilities of military families. I missed connecting with them because of the realities of our immediate family needs. I continued my education and received a BA in Journalism/Public Relations from the University of Central Florida in 1995. Throughout the years, I have continued my professional development

efforts by being connected and joining Meeting Planners International, attending training classes, and working with other professionals. I am currently working on my MBA with a concentration in Hospitality and Tourism from Strayer University.

I have always enjoyed working and have excelled in my professional endeavors because I was able to recognize my skills and work through challenges.

Four Regular Habits to Overcome Challenges

1. **Be Spiritually Centered:** Taking time out to listen.
2. **Not Sweating the Small Stuff:** I always felt that if no one is deathly ill or dying, that whatever is happening is just a process or phase in life—it's not the end.
3. **Find the Good in and Remember the Good in Whatever the Challenge Might Be:** You learn and grow from what the lesson was—and if you don't get it, you'll keep doing the same thing repeatedly.
4. **Realize Your Blessings:** In order to move forward, you must remember where you came from. This helps you understand where you are and where you are headed.

What happened after your husband retired?

In my search to further my career after military life, I was looking for an opportunity where I could be a business owner, and still be focused on my family and things that were important to my lifestyle. I also wanted to do something that was of interest to me. I love to travel and I love planning events. In my search, I found all of that and more with HelmsBriscoe, global meeting procurement company.

I wanted to be part of something that could help me determine my own destiny. There is mutual support from my counterparts and I am enjoying the lifestyle and success that my choice of working with HelmsBriscoe offers.

It's really a partnership. Many of the clients who use us wonder where we have been, as we are able to pass on the strength of a global organization and its benefits to companies to whom these types of benefits would be out of reach.

Are you a travel agent?

No, I'm more than a travel agent. I'm intimate with my clients' programs. I'm the central point who knows and grows with the meeting planner and the programs—I'm an extension of their planning team.

So, what do you actually do?

I help clients in all industries, from CEOs to admins, save time and money when planning a meeting. Whether it's the eleventh hour and they needed a location yesterday, or planning 10 years in advance, I find the right location at the right price, personally packaged and delivered, all at no cost to the client.

I ensure that my clients have memorable, valuable, and educational experiences for their meetings, functions, and events.

Because our organization is so well respected in the hospitality industry, I have access to resources like preferred rates, concessions, and up-to-date industry news that can benefit my clients. I am able to leverage buying power, negotiate favorable contract terms, and build great relationships to create success for clients and the hospitality industry as a whole.

With so many global changes, are people still traveling to meetings?

The hospitality industry is really changing—which affects many businesses. In the past, we could count on longer-term contracts booked further out. With changes in the economy, increased technological capabilities, and decreased staffing and budgets, businesses are cutting back on travel-related expenditures. However, there is no replacing face-to-face communication and camaraderie to keep people motivated and connected.

Everyone is adjusting and what we're noticing is:

- More short-term bookings
- A decrease in the length of meetings
- Meeting planners are combining several smaller meetings with larger ones

These factors validate the value of the types of services we provide because once a client makes a decision to hold a meeting, they have less time to plan, are often more cost conscious, and still need quality, value, and excellent service. I provide those things.

Benefits of working with me:

Personalized service—I do the legwork for meeting planners, giving them more time to focus on meeting content and ultimately produce a more impactful experience for attendees. It's like having an operations manager at no cost to the client.

Get Connected with Deborah Shorter at
dshorter@helmsbriscoe.com.

Section Two
THE MAP

Business Planning and Operating Strategies

Chief Executive Authority

*"Wisdom is the principle thing; therefore get wisdom:
and with all thy getting, get understanding."*
Proverbs 4:7

Successful Living from Jo Lena Johnson

There are five main areas of life that are concerns for most people—
meaning that the things that are priorities in most of our lives can
usually be grouped into these categories. I've found the "grouping" to
be a pretty good approach to focusing on what's important, releasing
what's not important, and to focusing on opportunities for growth
and development.

The Five Main Areas of Successful Living

1. Health
2. Work/Education
3. Relationships/Family
4. Finances
5. Spirituality/Community

You can use these categories to determine what you do want versus
what you don't want when choosing your priorities. Each of us, at
times, has given space to things like stress, tension, poor health,
frustration, poverty, or any other challenges you may be facing now.

What do you really want? For you? For your life? For your family? For your future? And, what are you willing to do in order to get there? Sometimes, it's a matter of just knowing where to start, and, of course, how to finish!

Operating as an Authority:
Questions and Considerations

Leadership from Jo Lena Johnson

Do you know what you really want?

Can you share that vision with yourself and others in a way that they "get it"? In a way that's clear to you and anyone else who is affected by the vision?

- Are you willing to focus single-mindedly on purpose-driven good works, whatever the method, channel, or opportunity for growth, even when challenging?

- Do you show yourself and others respect by being personable, articulate, trustworthy, and appreciative of the differences— even when you don't want to be or it doesn't feel good?

- Are you serious enough to study, and to listen to sound wisdom? Are you willing to seek out guidance and to question what's easy to see, and what may be missing?

- Are you courageous enough to stand up for your own morals, values, judgments, and standards, and for those of others who may not know, may not understand, or who simply may not care?

- Are you in touch with your primary resources?

Your thoughts, time, talent, and feelings are those precious resources that, once dwindled, are very difficult for you to restore by yourself.

- What are the areas that get the most attention from you? What are the areas wherein lies the most opportunity for growth?

In my leadership classes, I ask these questions and more. When you think about the five primary areas of concern for your life, begin to consider what you are doing to contribute to or to take away from what is most important to you. What do you really care about?

The reality is that most managers, supervisors, and business owners have not had leadership training. To successfully run a business takes courage, awareness, and overcoming considerations. What you do and sa, don't do and say, and what you show makes a difference. As an entrepreneur, you are the model and the mold. How do I spell successful? Y-O-U!

Filling in the Gaps with a Purple Basket

"I'll always be learning—(having) someone who can shed light on where I'm going and where I'd like to be, is a great reason to get a business coach."

Insight from Angel Were

What is your vision for your company, "The Purple Basket"?

My vision is to be known throughout the U.S. and globally. We take into consideration who you are buying for; we ask questions about the person and create a customized basket that really means something to the person receiving it.

Why did you choose that name?

I wanted people to know that we specialize in baskets and purple has always been my favorite color.

Why did you start your business?

In 1996, during my freshman year Morehead State University in Morehead, Kentucky, students would get care packages delivered to them at the dorm. I observed that only some students were on the list to get care packages with treats in them.

I thought it would be great if all students could get care packages, especially around midterms and finals, because it would boost their confidence and be a show of support during stressful times.

Since there were more students passing by than care packages, I thought it was a way I could help students feel good about themselves.

Throughout the years, I have taken basket-making classes and received some certifications. Now that I've honed skills through education and experience, I've become a wife and mother, and I wanted to use my creativity by doing what I enjoy. So, in March 2008, I started The Purple Basket as my entrepreneurial pursuit.

What are some benefits of your business?

1. **My customers benefit:** They have the ability to choose what they like, and I work with them to provide options of what they would need for a gift.
2. **I benefit and feel fulfilled:** Being able to visualize a gift and to complete an order or request is fulfilling to me, and is hopefully pleasing to the recipient of The Purple Basket because it is filled with personalized items meant especially for them.
3. **My happiness benefits my family:** We are all happy because my business gives me a balance—since I like doing it, I am in my element and my children and family benefit because I'm more satisfied, flexible, adaptable, and fulfilled.
4. **Working with other business owners produces growth, expansion, and additional resources:** I collaborate with others; the exchange of information and ideas becomes valuable not just for one person but for each of us.

What are your goals for your business?

To attain corporate contracts with wedding planners, event planners, real estate companies, or colleges and universities, and to develop a network of professional businesses in which I can incorporate their products in my baskets. Relationship building is very important with The Purple Basket.

I want to deliver excellent customer service, following up in a timely manner and fulfilling their orders as requested.

How do you market your business?

By attending networking events; having daily conversations with people in places like the grocery store; by reading the newspaper; and contacting people and offering my services as a raffle or giveaway prize for their events.

What does "success" mean to you?

When you have reached the pre-determined goal(s), and keep going, setting new ones along the way and working toward them, because goals should change with attainment.

There is always room for improvement. Keep going on all levels—not just financial—it has many components: your personality, your spirituality, your financial status. It's who you are; it makes you the person you are supposed to be.

What are five questions you have about becoming a "successful entrepreneur?"

Angel asks:

1. How do you do it? Specifically, who do you contact?
2. How do you go about contacting (that) someone, getting through the gatekeeper, and reaching the person you need to speak with, as a small (one-person show) business?
3. How do you do what you need to do with limited resources?
4. How can I find someone who can help me work through the accounting matters like taxes, benefits, and such, while I'm still trying to create the finances to afford them?
5. How do you go about finding a coach and a mentor?

Jo Lena replies: These are great questions and thanks for asking them because others probably have similar ones. We'll answer some in the book, and hopefully, some of our readers will Get Connected! with you as well.

Now, we'll answer question(s) with a question… Why would you like a coach?

Because I don't know it all and I would like to have someone help me, to answer questions in a reciprocating relationship. I'll always be learning, and having someone who can shed light on where I'm going and where I'd like to be would help me create a strong foundation for what I really want.

Why a mentor?

Having a mentor always helps for accountability—assistance along the way helps you obtain your goals more efficiently and more realistically.

What are the top four challenges you have faced as a woman business owner?

1. Lack of financial resources
2. Marketing is expensive
3. Time management—figuring out how to schedule things and manage things while having a family
4. Making the best decisions with my time to obtain new customers.

What are three resources that, if you had them, would help you reach more students who deserve to have a purple basket?

1. I want to create partnerships with colleges and universities in Missouri. There are many events in which my service could be used, especially to notify parents of where they can obtain student care packages.
2. Real estate agencies bringing in new agents—they are always looking to give gifts to their would-be homeowner clients— they need gift baskets.
3. Holiday parties—teachers are already overloaded and being able to provide gift baskets for them and their students would be really good for everyone.

Get Connected with Angel at
www.thepurplebasket.com or by emailing her at
angel@thepurplebasket.com.

Five Things Every Woman Interested in Business Should Know

*"Work in the same industry you want to go into—
that way you learn what not to do."*

Wisdom from Tessa Greenspan

Tessa Greenspan is the former president and CEO of Sappington Farmers Market in St. Louis, Missouri. She was nominated as one of the America's Most Influential Business Connectors for the U.S. Small Business Administration, among numerous awards including the SBA's Small Business Person of the Year for the Saint Louis region, and was chosen one of the Top 25 Most Influential Women in Saint Louis by the St. Louis Business Journal. She is one of the most successful women we actually know! Her goal is to contribute and touch as many lives as possible and to make a real difference.

What Donna loves about Tessa Greenspan:

"Her attitude! She always has smile on her face—always has a big hug for me—a word of encouragement—has influenced me to be warm, welcoming, and to give hugs. Ten years ago, in corporate America, you didn't go up and hug someone. Now, even at networking events you see hugging going on all the time."

Before Starting a Business, What are Five Things Every Business Woman Should Know?

Tessa says, *"There are so many things…"*

1. **When you are starting off, do your due diligence.** There is so much you really need to know, so research to find out if what you are attempting to provide is sustainable or a flash in the pan. Consider trends, competition, location, and the price points of similar products or services. There are so many considerations before you even get off the ground. Also, consider your target audience, your marketing plan, and where you will network. These are a few of the many things to consider. If you work for another company, you can get a lot of those answers.

2. **Interview someone who is successful in that business or similar business.** Avoid heartache by preventing as many mistakes as you can. Mistakes are costly and avoiding pitfalls through experienced wisdom is a great investment of your time. Most successful people are glad to share things they have done. Find someone locally or in another area of the country by asking for an interview. Include questions about recommendations for moving forward in addition to things they would do differently if they could start again.

3. **Counsel.** Get the best lawyer, accountant, and banker that you can—don't scrimp! Meet with them on a quarterly basis—these relationships are so important to building a solid foundation.

4. **Get Sufficient Capital.** Always expect that it will take more money and more time to become profitable—don't go in on a shoestring. That's why so many businesses fail because they don't have the capital.

5. **Treat your employees as if they are your most cherished, prized customer.** It is the most overlooked and one of the most important things you can do. If you value people, they feel good about themselves and they will respond positively. If the people who work for you are happy, and they know that they are making a difference, it transcends into how they treat the customers.

   How you present things makes a huge difference. One of the ways I showed appreciation at the food market (similar to Whole Foods) was to get on the PA system and say "Pam gets a candy bar and a star for good customer service." By announcing to everyone, publicly, it told the customers that we appreciated them as well. When you compliment people, it develops that type of atmosphere in the store or the business. When you need to share feedback that is not particularly favorable, always share it privately—never publicly, because it will embarrass them and they will never forget it. It also impedes them from trying again.

Tessa says, "If I could do it all again, I would act quicker when something wasn't going well—in other words, I would cut the cord quicker." At times, I allowed negative people to be in the space too long. It's not helpful to anyone to have negative people, people who aren't happy in their space or people who are not interested as part of the organization or team. Negativity can be like a cancer and it affects others. "The most important thing is to do what you know is right. Go with your gut—when you know something is right—do it—don't carry on and on."

More than simply well informed and successful, Tessa is "great." She is great because she is experienced, knows who she is, what she has to offer, and is willing to share her wisdom, experience, and time with people—openly and genuinely. Her goal in life is to live full out, healthy, and to touch as many people in a positive way as possible. She also has a goal of helping at least a dozen women earn a six-figure and beyond residual income.

Tessa is known as the "Queen of Juice" and is developing another health and wellness business with products that are anti-inflammatory, anti-aging, and natural botanicals which balance your metabolic system, and she'll be glad to support you.

Get Connected with Tessa at
Tessagreenspan@aol.com.

Four Keys to Building a Solid Business Foundation

"When investing in your business do not use the equity in your home and do not use credit cards."

Strategies from Donna Gamache

I have learned so much during my years as a business owner. One of the biggest lessons happened when I jumped into a partnership without doing the legwork. In other words, I didn't take time to learn what a partnership involved and how to build a strong partnership.

When investing in your business don't use the equity in your home and don't use credit cards. If you are a small home-based business, you may want to consider keeping your full-time job while you build the foundation of your business. Alternatively, keep your expenses to a minimum and pay as you go. Once you have a product or service and have built the solid foundation, there are angel investors who may be able to help with funding your business.

1. **Define your business idea and create a clear and concise mission statement.** You need to articulate this to everyone so that they understand what you offer in 30 words or less. Sounds tough, right? It is possible with coaching and practice. Your mission statement should be the foundation upon which your business is built.

2. **Create a solid business plan.** This can be intimidating to most people but it doesn't have to be complicated and shouldn't have everything in it. You can keep it simple because your operating document will contain more details. You must however, have a one-page business plan so that anyone can read it and see the direction of your business. Get connected at www.onepagebusinessplan.com as a good start.

3. Create a solid marketing plan for investors.

- Identify your customers
- Identify customer needs
- Share how you will provide the needed products/services
- Share how you intend to communicate with your customers
- Provide a measurable sales plan to track success/results
- Provide your back up plan if "plan A" doesn't work

4. Do research.

- Are there other companies that do the same thing you do?
- Who are your competitors, and what makes you different?
- Collaborate with other small businesses in your area. Oftentimes the power of collective thought and action is what will help you succeed.

S.C.O.R.E. is an organization made up of retired business people who can help you write your business and marketing plan. Find out what else you need for your particular product or service at www.score.org. Get Connected to the dedicated sector supporting women entrepreneurs at www.score.org/women.

Good Credit: a Woman's Best Friend

"Choose a bank big enough to handle all of your business needs but small enough to remember who you are."

Wisdom from Pam Ross

Why is having a good relationship with your banker so important?

Pam Ross replies:

1. If you are able to set up a line of credit, do so before you need it because once you actually need it, no bank will give it to you.

2. You need the banker to have some notion of what type of person you are; to make a judgment about you, your ethics, and your logic; it's an emotional connection that a credit report can't always relay to someone (although a good credit score is a woman's best friend).

3. Internally, bankers know that real estate collateral doesn't make payments. They would prefer cash collateral. If you really want to have a line of credit, save some cash, and put it in the bank. Borrowing your own money is the cheapest way to get a loan. The bank isn't risking anything because they have your money, and you develop a credit relationship.

Even if it's a small amount like $2,500 or $5,000 it will be well worth it because:

    a.   You'll get the lowest possible interest rate

    b.   You improve your credit score

    c.   They will trust you more because you've shared the risk with them, thus improving your relationship

Relationships take time to develop

The decision of where to bank is extremely important in terms of what you need. Choose a bank big enough to handle all of your business needs, but small enough to remember who you are.

A better relationship means you'll probably get better service and you want somebody to know who you are. You don't want to be anonymous. That's one of the problems with the big banks—you are anonymous to them.

Pick a bank that suits your business needs; it's more than location. Choose a locally owned, stable regional bank with low employee turnover.

The best way is to use the line of credit and pay it down; use it and pay it down.

You work inside of a corporate structure, have you always done that?

No, I'm an "Interpreneur"

An "Interpreneur" is essentially someone who is building a business inside of an existing business. It's the difference between someone who can walk a high wire without a net and someone who can do the same thing with a net. I need the net.

I'm a creative person inside a stable business who listens to my creative ideas and it gives me flexibility. I've been a business owner in the past and I couldn't tolerate the risk. I really didn't have the money to withstand the distance between the paycheck and my investment. I ran out of money, I had family responsibilities, and it's just too scary.

I was self-employed a lot. It's not exactly the same thing; it's being a consultant—getting the work because you can see the path.

Get Connected to Pam Ross
at Peoples National Bank in Clayton, Missouri,
at 314.726.7330.
She's a long-time BNI member
because it's a successful way to generate referrals.

Go Getters Get Results!

"At times, some business owners can be cowards because they don't want to make the tough decisions about people."

Performance Improvement Strategies from Kathy Boas, SPHR

Kathy Boas says:

When I see something I really want, I go after it. When starting my business I didn't know anything about how to start it, so I went out and found the people, the tools, and the resources to start and grow my business.

What services do you provide?

I support business owners in various aspects of performance improvement, retention and profitability, training, strategic development, and general human resources advice and counsel.

What insights can you share with our business owners about performance improvement needs affecting them and their employees?

I believe that if they don't have the right person in the right position, they won't be successful. Employers need to understand how critical it is to hire the right people for the right jobs, train them effectively, and then let them do the job they were hired to do!

Six Reasons for Broken Organizations and Poor Results

1. The wrong person is in the job.

2. They (the owner) are not willing to let go of the reins and give the employee the opportunity to innovate in the position.

3. They overlook those employees who are best qualified to be able to carry on the mission and the company's strategic goals.

4. You need the right people in the right jobs in the right company, and if you don't have that, you don't have anything but a broken organization.

5. They don't recognize the significant cost and loss of productivity to the business if employees aren't trained and retained.

6. They haven't clearly communicated job and performance expectations to employees.

In your experience, why do owners allow poor performance?

Business Owners Don't Pay Attention!

1. Sometimes they are making money so, "If it ain't broke, don't fix it."

2. They surround themselves with "yes" people.

3. They can be cowards because they don't want to make the tough decisions about people.

4. They can be egotistical.

5. They can be narrow-minded.

6. They just don't know, what they don't know.

If you really want to be successful in managing and expanding your business, please do some self-reflection. If you have adopted any of these habits, take some time to weigh your ego against your potential success.

Small businesses hopefully grow into profitable large organizations when the leader takes action. If you are unsure how to fix or improve something, people like me are here to help you.

Four Growth Strategies for Small Businesses

1. Take the time to hire the right people.

2. Once they have started, invest in their development.

3. Find out what motivates them because no two people are alike.

   When I hire someone, I ask her or him for the top three things that motivate them. They can't say money or promotion—they must name other things like movie tickets, event passes, or educational opportunities. For some people it's nothing more than telling them they did a good job. It can be so easy if you really take the time to find out.

4.   If you have the right people doing the right job in the right company, they will be motivated and engaged. They will want to do the best for their internal customers (co-workers), for themselves and for their external customers/clients!

Relationships based on mutual respect and mutual trust serve everyone and improve business profitability. Believe me, this works… it's amazing.

Why did you start your business?

I was a divorced single mom. During the first 6 months, I looked for a new position, but since I knew business and human resources I thought I could leverage my talents and take some consulting opportunities during that time. After 6 month, it was clear to me that I needed to focus on finding a full-time position or on starting this business.

I was going in two different directions and what I finally realized is that where I found my true calling was in consulting. I like the idea of being able to go in and troubleshoot issues and make an organization stronger and more profitable, and the people happier. It's that nurturing kind of thing: "How can I help you?" is my way of living.

So I worked with Art Donnelley, my CPA, and Mike Collins, a former client with whom I had done outplacement. Mike was also a marketing guru. On Mike's recommendation, I then started working on how to get more PR—which is free marketing.

Between Art, Mike, and me, we established a relationship that allowed me to put together a business plan, a budget, cover letters, marketing letters, and materials, and prepared me for cold calls. You name it, we all did it.

How did you get PR without spending money?

I wrote for various publications like the *Kansas City Business Journal, Ingram's,* and the *Small Business Monthly.* I did speaking engagements for a variety of associations and professional groups, and I offered some free business workshops. I also created relationships with some of the local TV reporters so that when they had stories about various business topics like Workplace Violence, Professional Dress, or Interviewing Techniques, they would call me. If I wasn't an expert in that topic, I would refer them to some really good people.

As a result, my business grew—in fact, it grew so much that I purchased another company and merged it with my business. I then sold it after 10 years with a sizable profit, and I went to work for other consulting companies.

With all of that success, why did you sell the business?

I was tired of the selling. I was very unhappy to the point that my staff recognized it and I also recognized it in terms of my client relationships. I found that I was getting short with some of them, to the point where I had to call them back and apologize. This wasn't me!

How did you find someone to buy your business, and what happened as a result?

I started putting the word out in the community that I was thinking of selling it. I had lunch with a competitor and explained what I was I doing, and we both decided to merge my business with theirs. I had six people on staff at the time and they all found other positions. Not one of them was out of work. I sold the equipment to another consultant who was expanding her business. It was a God thing; it was amazing, the timing, and the ease that we closed the transaction. The new company got my book of business as well as my services as a consultant.

What it took from me to sell my business:

1. It took soul searching to realize that I didn't want to be a business owner anymore, nor did I want the responsibilities of having employees.
2. I talked with my employees and supported them in finding other positions.
3. I looked at my book of business and considered the needs of every client to make sure they would receive excellent customer service during the transition. By the way, I didn't lose one client when I made the transition to my new firm.
4. Because I had taken out an SBA loan, I went through my financials to see if I could pay the loan off early, in 3 years versus 5 years. After looking at my expenses and income, I was able to pay off the loan in 3 years.
5. I picked a company with a philosophical focus and values that I have. Integrity was important, which is why I passed up other companies who had been interested but didn't offer those values, in my opinion.

It was an easy transition—when you have a consulting company people think you have a lot of freedom, and that's not necessarily true. It wasn't traumatic for me because I had made the decision that I didn't want to have my own business anymore. However, although there were some legal bumps, the transition wasn't that difficult.

I worked for the firm for two years, then the company was purchased, and they decided not to offer consulting services. So in effect, my job was eliminated.

After that position was eliminated, what did you do next?

A former colleague of mine working with another firm, was looking for someone with my skill set, including my sales experience. I was there for 2 years and unfortunately, it wasn't the right fit. It got to the point where I could be fired or quit at any moment. So before I resigned, I brought in another $20K project, which I was able to see through completion.

About 2 weeks after I had left my position, one of my long-term clients, a printing company, created a new position for me and hired me as their administrative manager. After about 1 ½ years, it became clear that I had worked myself out of a job. Both the president of the company and I knew it, so we parted on good terms (the company is still one of my clients). That was in November of 2005 and I went back into the job market. In 2 years I took two positions, which were not right for me—good companies but wrong positions.

In 2007, I went back into consulting. Boas Associates is open for business. I have come full circle, and I do not have any sales responsibilities in my current consulting role. For that, I am grateful.

Most of the work I do now comes from referrals. I'm also adjunct staff at Metropolitan Community College and I'm a performance management consultant for Right Management. I'm just a "Jackie" of all trades…

Get Connected with Kathy at
kboas_50@msn.com.

Five Traits of Good Customer Service

"In order to be successful, you must like dealing with people."

Wisdom from Dawn Conner

Five Traits of Good Customer Service

1. Follow-up
2. Problem solving
3. Being detail oriented
4. Organizing
5. Servicing/tending to people by meeting their needs

Major Skills Needed to Be Successful in Customer Service

- Be flexible.
- You have to like dealing with people because they are going to call (on) you. When listening to someone, you can tell if the person is tired, tired that day, or tired of doing it (giving good customer service).
- Use common sense. When you see errors, such as things in error on orders, as a representative you cannot just run with it. It might be worth delaying the order to get clarification on what is happening in the process.

Dawn Conner continues:

When I go to work, I'm figuratively on stage; I'm in a performance from the time I get there until the time I leave. It *really* helps to deal with some of the things that are going on. Still, many companies look at customer service as a meaningless task. However, many companies go under because they have poor customer service.

In order to be successful, you must like dealing with people. And, if you don't have the mindset, you will not survive. It takes survival skills because you will not learn about customer service in school. I don't think there is a customer service degree or customer service training in school, but thank God for my INROADS training. I'm also grateful for having the opportunity to work for a company before beginning my actual corporate career.

About INROADS: We spent four summers learning professional development skills including organizational strategies, interviewing skills, time management, and other crucial skills. Since the internship happened throughout our college experience, it prepared us for the corporate environment and that "corporate experience"—which can be something—and not everyone survives it.

Dawn Conner currently works in corporate America and has spent most of her life in the field of customer service. She is passionate and knows how to establish rapport, create solutions, solve problems, and how to build relationships through challenges.

As a business owner, please be aware of your attitude, temperament, and focus when it comes to your customers and your business—you too, are "figuratively on stage."

Setting Your Business on Fire

"Until you extend your gift to the people you are meant to serve—you will never live a full life and they will never know why something is missing."

Strategic Coaching from Monikah Ogando

Branded by her students and clients as The Business Explosion Coach™, Monikah Ogando is the founder and CEO of Ogando Associates, LLC, a business coaching and training firm which was named to the *Inc 500*, an exclusive ranking of the nation's fastest-growing private companies. Monikah has created a dynamic enterprise that is devoted to creating financial freedom around the world. Through the power of entrepreneurship, Monikah helps thousands of members start and grow their own businesses.

How do you help people grow their businesses?

I work with entrepreneurs who are really passionate and good at what they do but who may not know how to create compelling marketing campaigns or how to set up systems so they ALWAYS attract clients. My workshops, home-study courses, and coaching programs are specifically designed so my students and clients put systems in place within a few months (sometimes days or weeks). This leads to getting the quality and amount of clients they really need—quickly.

There are many coaches around. What sets you apart from others?

1. I'm a no-nonsense coach. I'm not interested in processing people and their history. I focus on what their goal is and what's the fastest way to get there.
2. I'm very clear that you can be a millionaire with the skills and talents you already have—you don't have to go out and become something that you are not.
3. We are all here to serve humanity so I don't work with people who are just about greed and have a "let me make as much money as possible mentality" at the expense of others, or their own integrity. That doesn't align with what I'm up to.

What are five things you _really_ want entrepreneurs to know?

1. You have a unique gift for this planet.
2. You can be outrageously wealthy by living into and extending that gift.
3. There are people in this world that <u>you exclusively</u> are meant to touch.
4. There are techniques and strategies to do that in the shortest amount of time with maximum impact—your job as an entrepreneur is to uncover and leverage them.
5. Until you extend your gift to the people you are meant to serve—you will never live a full life and they will never know why something is missing.

Seven Quick Steps People Can Take to Get on Track

1. Get crystal clear on what you want to create. You must be able to answer a yes or no question. Either you made six figures or you didn't.

2. Develop structures and environments that pull you forward. Sometimes we push ourselves to do something, and it feels forced. However, when you develop an accountability structure, like a coach or a mastermind team, this automatically begins to pull you toward your greatness, instead of you having to push yourself or force yourself there.

3. Find a mentor and model those people who have already achieved the success you want. Find a mentor or coach who has already generated what you want to generate—and stick with them. Read their books. Enroll in their program. Follow their process because they have already blazed that trail and traveled the path. So you don't have to reinvent the wheel.

4. Make decisions based on where you are headed—not where you are afraid you'll end up. For example, if you want to build a media empire like Oprah's—ask yourself "What would Oprah do here?" Make sure that each decision will take you where you want to go.

5. Release habits, environments, and people that don't support your vision. The successes I've gotten have been more about what I've released rather than what I've taken on.

6. Close all back doors—eliminate all excuses. We are very soft on ourselves about our future and very hard on ourselves about our past. I want people to be soft on your past— get out of guilt and shame and be disciplined, focused, and unrelenting about the future you are creating. In other words, flip the switch.

7. Step into your vision now. Be it now. The reason you have that vision is that on some level, it's already done and already handled. All you've got to do is step into it.

I often hear many entrepreneurs say "I don't have time to plan or strategize, I need to make money." What do you say to that?

Although many times people say they want to make money, money in and of itself is never the end result. We want money for something: For some it's security or safety. For others, money represents freedom. So when you are clear about what the ultimate prize is for you, then the "how" can shift because the "why" is so big and juicy that you can redesign yourself to have it happen.

What is the goal for your business at this time? My goal is to touch and empower thousands of entrepreneurs to design their businesses in a way that honors who they are and the lifestyle they want to lead.

For example, someone might love to travel internationally and want to do so to spread her or his message. That means they have to design a platform for their message that is wide reaching—and one of the most effective ways is through publishing their book and launching a speaking career. And so, what I do as a coach is to get them clear on what they want their life to look like—and then we design the business to fund that life.

What are the five ways you are doing that?

1. **Get clear on what my market wants from me and give it to them:** My students and clients want interactivity with me— so I engage in a dialog with them. This is great because it means I'm not always the sole content generator. When I'm clear about what my target market wants from me, I deliver

it in a way that best addresses their needs. Yes, they want skills and to learn, but they also want a place where they can hone their own skills and that's what the Mastermind Inner Circle membership provides for them.

2. **Logistics:** Coaching products are available for purchase and download on my website and have been designed with my target market in mind. I'm clear about what problem I'm solving for them and what promise I'm delivering on. That helps me to craft my sales copy on the site, helps me to craft my offer and helps me to design the content of what I'm actually delivering—so I know how to deliver the content.

3. **Creating strategic alliances with influencers and experts in my field:** For example, the last three people that enrolled in my Mastermind Inner Circle program did so because of the interview I did with David Mathison, author of "Be The Media." Since he's a well-known expert in his field, connecting with him further established my own credibility. So my market gets to see that I'm up to big things and they want to come and play here.

*Play—whatever you are up to, take action on it and create results—every goal. If I look at my business like a game, every game has a team (could be competition, rules, scores) so, here's how to win the game, here's how to score, here's the team I am playing against, then I can go out there and play a championship game to win.

We are a week away from the Super Bowl—the New Orleans Saints are going into uncharted territory because they've never been a Super Bowl contender. So they are doing research now: they need to know their strengths, weaknesses, resources that they have to make winning easier. When I am coaching my clients and students on designing a business game they want to win, I am helping them establish those parameters—and now the plan to win the game almost becomes obvious.

4. **Being generous in my visibility:** A lot of folks talk about using social media (Twitter, Facebook, YouTube, and blogging, for example, which I consider to be the main four pillars for online visibility right now). It's tempting to start putting out messages that say, "Go to my website and buy" or "Come to my event," but people don't want to buy from you; they want to be served by you. So I give them tips, I give them strategies, I am giving them resources they didn't know existed, and I'm speaking to a secret conversation they may have but are not holding in a public forum.

   For example, it's very common for leaders, authors, and speakers to always be positive—look at the win, the visibility—it's not looked upon with respect or trust when you share your struggles publicly. But when I address those secret conversations, then the people I'm working with see me as relatable. They see they can trust me. They begin to think, "Wow, she knows things about me that I don't have to explain to her." In a way, it helps them save face a little and not be or feel like they are being judged.

5. Bringing it back to center: **I get to be authentic to my values, my desired lifestyle and to myself.** I want to be more available to my family, to freely choose to not have to touch the computer for a couple of days or a week, and my business keeps running smoothly and profitable whether I'm front and center or not. When I'm authentic in realizing that, then I align my business and my goals in a way that

Do you actually do design work?

Yes, we can take an existing logo or introduce a brand new logo—my marketing/graphics designer will help me to work with the client to create it or tweak it.

What are Five Things People Really Need to Know About Branding?

1. **Your branding needs to identify who you are.** If that's text or logo, it should have some form of tag line that is attached to the logo or with the logo itself, which says everything.

    For example, GMS represents Gladys M. Schubach, GMS Incentives (my company name) represents "Great Merchandise Selection," and we also offer "Great Manufacturing Services." By the time I've had a conversation, they'll know and will retain GMS along with my tag line, "Your One Stop Source." When they look at my website they will think, "Gee, I can get anything, because GMS Incentives really is "Your One Stop Source."

2. **The branding of your name must be consistent.** This includes tag lines, premium products, and your verbal presentation when meeting or interacting with clients.

3. **Keep it simple.** I'm a firm believer that less is more. Leave them with a simple message so they will retain it.

    For example, if my parting message to you was, "We do branding, marketing, premium, and promotional products, logo design, awards, embroidery" on and on, then when

I leave you, you may be thinking, "What was her name again?" or "What was her company name?"

However, if we've had good interaction and I leave you with "GMS Incentives, Your One Stop Source" it will be intriguing enough for you to want to know more.

4. **"Dripping" is extremely important.** It means consistent exposure and contact with your prospects or clients. Continually connecting with and nurturing your clients with your branding, message, services, and product offerings.

Key factors are consistent branding—be it blogs, social networking sites, emails, newsletters, or premium items. You get to show them the breadth and depth of what you offer.

Through these forms of communication, dripping allows you to slowly unfold the various products and services you can offer your client. Many times people will go to a competitor and buy a product or service from them because they didn't know that you offered that service.

5. **Listen to your client—prospect.** They will communicate how they like to make their buys. Some people are so quick in going in to sell themselves and what they offer, they lose their focus or purpose. End result: the client is not heard and their needs aren't fulfilled.

By listening to your client, you will recognize the best form of communication for them. When you listen, you will be able to interpret their needs and offer a course of action that will work well for them.

For example, I have some people who say they don't do email. That means that they want everything in hard copy format—flyers, correspondence—via mail and catalogs.

Another client may say that they are overwhelmed and that their desk is cluttered with paper. That means that they want email correspondence, links to product selection, and quarterly flyers or promotions sent electronically.

Finally, always keep in mind the 80/20 Rule. Twenty percent of your client base will generate eighty percent of your business. Identify the clients who are consistently partnering with you. Focus on them!

2010 marks the tenth year anniversary of GMS Incentives. I started the company because I love helping people by offering promotional marketing solutions that can help them grow their business. I take great pride in finding creative solutions that solve clients' needs. Exhaustive research is a major part of this effort. When I worked in TV, I had to do research on various businesses to seek out potential clients. When I began my incentives business I secured the largest frozen food manufacturer in the world as a client because I was able to create and implement a custom product for them within 10 months—something that my predecessor had not been able to do in 17 years.

GMS Incentives has maintained a referral-based business through all these years because I partner with my clients. In other words, I tie in who and what I know with what my clients really need—long-lasting, effective, and memorable exposure that helps them grow their businesses. At GMS Incentives, we really are "Your One Stop Source."

Gladys really is "Your One Stop Source." She has been extremely instrumental in spreading "good" throughout her years in business, as well as providing really good products for the "If You Really Want to ..." series.

Get Connected with Gladys at
www.GMSincentives.com.

Viral Marketing Solidifies Your Future

*"1.8 billion people shop online and it's never gone down.
74.4% of the North American population is online."*

Wisdom from Peggy McColl

Peggy McColl shares:

The Top Three Reasons Learning the Process of Viral Marketing is Crucial to Business Owners in This Day and Age

1. The main reason is the way business is conducted with rapid and continued growth. Consumers are behaving differently, so businesses need to adjust. We're in business to make money and to create relationships—be they long term or short lived. If you're not online today and you're not using the Internet to support or expand your brand and visibility, you are losing opportunity and the ability to connect.

2. For instance, taking your dog to the groomers… The paper version of Yellow Pages is out of date after it's shipped out because it's not updated on a regular basis like the Internet. Go to the Internet and type in "dog groomer," and even if they just opened up last month, then you would find them provided they are online and have a website.

3. For business people you have to be online and if you are
    not, you are missing out on business. You become labeled or
    thought of as someone who is behind the times.

1.8 billion people shop online and it's never gone down. 74.4% of
the North American population is online.

You don't have to be technical. Many online programs and services
often work intuitively because they anticipate the way human beings
think.

If you are not on social media and creating or posting videos, and
recognized as someone who has video today, you will be behind the
times.

I wanted to learn how to create videos myself and found someone
who teaches people and charges reasonable rates. I wanted to create
an iMovie, so I opened up the program, and without any training
I looked at the tutorial. Last night I posted a little movie I created.

I bought images off iStock photos that I needed. I put them in
sequence and posted it. I also created a web page and added it to my
site through using "Website Tonight" from GoDaddy.com.

There are so many utilities available. Just typing into the browser
what you need caters to the learning experience; you must be patient
and willing to do things you wouldn't normally do. At times you
should hire experts to shave off time and teach you to do things that
you wouldn't normally do.

Your Destiny Switch

I love change; the Internet is constantly evolving and gives us a chance to grow more and do more.

Peggy McColl is a New York Times best-selling author and an internationally recognized expert in the field of self-help and Internet marketing. As an entrepreneur, business owner, mentor, and professional speaker, Peggy has been inspiring individuals to pursue their personal and business objectives.

She provides effective Internet marketing solutions for entrepreneurs, authors, publishers, professionals, and business owners, who want to establish an online presence, achieve bestseller status, build their brand, grow, and/or expand their business online.

Get Connected to Peggy at her website,
http://destinies.com.

Web Design Services and Your Online Presence

"I was the last one to figure it out ... I was supposed to be working for myself."

Wisdom from Susan Spencer

What is your current title?

I am a small business owner—president, owner, marketer, janitor, chief financial officer, chief marketing officer, and captain of my ship—and all of those other roles that one plays as an entrepreneur, of Spencer Web Design, Inc., and I've been in business for 7 years.

What is your educational background?

I hold a BA in Art. I didn't know what I wanted to do when I graduated high school and I always loved art. After graduating from Lindenwood University, I became a studio artist, which means that I was creating fine art in a studio—printmaking, ceramics, and stained glass.

I studied art history—and what intrigued me were the ideas that influenced style movements by artists. It made me appreciate the intellectual basis for trends—the why and how of what they did and when. Interestingly, I find the same process happening in business.

You've been described as a good friend. What does that mean to you?"

A "good friend" is someone who is helpful and caring. I have a good sense of humor and I'm friendly. I'm also an organizer—I like to put together lots of activities with my friends, dinners and things like that.

I like to connect people. I like to bring people together.

I value people—so if someone moves away, I try to stay in touch and maintain those relationships because I know that there is something of value there and I want to be sure that it continues. It's (friendship) a wonderful thing and I treasure being able to pick up where we left off—even if we haven't talked in a year.

How did Spencer Web Design, Inc. begin?

I didn't want to go into business, I never planned to be in business, and it seems that everything kept leading me to this.

I figured that I always wanted to be an employee and what I really wanted was just to be the boss. I loved working for small companies and through the years a couple of them closed and I had to move on. Each closing was emotional and disheartening. So, I went to work for a Fortune 500 company who had never laid off people in the 150 years of its existence. Fast forward to 9/11. My projects were put on hold and I was in the first round of lay-offs.

I still didn't understand that I was meant to have my own business and at the time, I had an opportunity to take a Dale Carnegie course—which I absolutely love and recommend for everyone. It became clear to me at the end of the 16-week course that I should be in business for myself. And then the owner said, "I'm glad you finally came to that because it was clear to me the first day that you were meant to be in business for yourself." If I had known, it would have saved me 16 weeks! (she says with a warm smile!)

While I was trying to figure it out, people started asking me to do work for them, and say things like, "Well, you do this, don't you?" and "Can you do this for me while you're off?" And no job that I applied for or saw advertised ever looked right—it didn't matter the title, the salary. *I was the last one to figure it out—and there was a reason I wasn't finding something working for someone else—I was supposed to be doing it for myself.*

The Four Most Rewarding Things about Being in Business

1. Being able to spend time with my son when he was younger was rewarding because being a single mom was really hard in the corporate world—being up so early and being gone for 12 hours a day.

2. Being able to say, "It's okay that I want to be the one who is in charge." I think that I always felt that it wasn't my place, I had a boss and it was their role to make decisions—I don't know why I thought that.

    Since I'm a natural organizer, I would notice things and opportunities to move forward and would want to implement them—but couldn't always do that because I wasn't the one in charge.

3. The variety has been very important. Meeting new people and finding out about new businesses has been very rewarding.

4. Knowing that I bring a lot to the table is beneficial to me and to my clients. My unique background gives my clients the benefit of my corporate experience and training plus the small business perspective, which would be lacking with others.

Five Steps to Greater Technological Communication

Understand what their (your customer or client's) pain is—and what you offer as a solution. Put yourself in your customer's shoes and really understand their concerns, the problems they are facing, and the reasons they are reaching out to you in the first place.

When formulating your online message:
1. Be clear
2. Be simple
3. Be precise
4. Understand what your prospect or customer is looking for
5. Understand how you are going to deliver (it)

Consider your Needs

If you are looking specifically for technological support, work with a professional who will listen to what's most important to you and to your needs. Consider limitations as well: your time, your capabilities, and if you want to or not want to deal with certain things—where you really want to focus your energy. Be sure that they educate you on the options—making recommendations so that you can make the best choices for you and your business.

What are Five "Don't Do's" for Business Owners when Considering Online Solutions?

1. **Don't do a "do it yourself website" when you don't have the knowledge and time to make it successful.** So many new businesses will create a situation where they are creating a bad first impression. The last thing people would do is call them—if the website looks bad, it makes them look bad— and they need to be aware of it right from the start.

2. **Don't think that you have to spend a lot of money to get a good start.** You can always do things in stages, if you lay the groundwork leading up to your ultimate goal, as long as each stage logically progresses into building toward the end result.

3. **Don't lose control of your online presence.** This includes owning your domain name, having access to your web files, hosting, and ownership of any and all of your web content.

4. **Don't do it all yourself.** Get objective input about what you are doing; understand that you may have limitations that you will not recognize for yourself. For instance, you may not think your logo is very important but it is such an important component of your brand that prospective clients will make judgments about you, based on what they see, starting with your logo.

    Get input from others when it comes to content, writing style, etc. This is about investing in your business and in your brand. If you don't show people the value in your brand then it will not build your business.

5. **Don't build it and forget—if you haven't touched your website in 5 years, don't ask why you aren't doing better.** Some large search engines like Google consider your site to be current only if it has been updated within the last 30 days.

Three Things I Really Want People to Know about Websites:

1. They are an extension of you and your business.

2. It's the front door that lets people in or keeps them out.

3. Choose a web designer who is reputable, with whom you have good communication, and who is capable of providing the options, choices, and flexibility that you need to develop your site in a way that makes sense for you.

I have heard so many horror stories about designers locking people out of their sites when they wanted to move them; about stealing domain names; and simply refusing to give access so that they can't transfer their sites away from them.

Integrity, commitment to representing you, your business and your best interests are extremely important and they can't be compromised, so please be sure to consider who you are working with before accepting a proposal—and be sure that the business has a proposal for you before trusting them with your online identity!

We offer a consulting relationship with our clients. We make sure there is a good fit so that they can get something of value from working with us. Sometimes people contact me for a website when they don't really need one—and I've had to turn them down... but there are still ways that I can help promote them online even without a website. This is especially important for entrepreneurs and start-ups, which may just be getting started and do not have a budget to put up a website. It's important for them to know we can still promote their business online without having a website. So, I encourage people to reach out and let us help them with the solutions they really need to accomplish their goals while building their businesses.

Our services include Web design and hosting,
eCommerce, and Search Engine Optimization.
Get Connected with Susan at
www.spencerwebdesign.com or email
info@spencerwebdesign.com.

Sales Tips for Growing Your Business

"You MUST eat at least one awful chicken lunch a week!"

Insights and Strategies from Sam Black

Although times are changing for sales, you can still do well! All it takes is some "elbow grease" applied to your business development activities. These tips are guaranteed to build the business you want. Make a promise to yourself that you will work on each of them over a 6-week time block so that by the end of the designated period, you will have all these channels working for you.

1. Ramp up your activities—all your activities. Whatever you did last year, double it! Double the number of dials you make each day. If you were doing 20 a day, now make 40 a day. If your goal was six appointments a week, aim for 12. If you are in one Chamber, make that two! Although your sales skills (quality) will be critical, in this economy success will also require QUANTITY. Fill that funnel!

2. You MUST eat at least one awful chicken lunch a week, preferably two. Go to different Chamber meetings and other networking meetings—as many as you can. You have to eat lunch, so why not with new people who might help you with your business? The more people you meet, the more opportunities to add to your database and build your referral network, which is critical.

3. Schedule at least ONE one-on-one coffee meeting each week, preferably two, with someone who can be a referral source for you and who you can help with their business. Spend some time thinking about who might be a direct referral source…someone in contact with the exact prospects that you need/want. Also, don't discount someone who is not in direct contact with your ideal prospect. That person knows other people who DO have direct contact—that person's spouse, clients/customers, other business associates, and friends. You'll be surprised where your next connection may come from. Be creative and be open to every possible contact source.

4. Join at least one new Chamber…a Chamber that is at least a 20-minute drive away from your normal networking neighborhood! Get out of your box. Meet people who may not ever have met you…and then schedule a coffee with those new people.

5. Build that database! If you haven't formally done it, this is the time to DO IT! Use a database application (ACT! or any other good program) that will allow you to implement drip marketing, that will create organized and targeted calling lists for you each day (so you can easily do your 40 dials), and that will allow you to send "blast' email messages. If you have a good prospect and customer database, keep adding to it. Fifty new names a week! I'm serious! That's 2400 new names a year, minimum! Add all those people you meet at networking events PLUS read your business section of the newspaper each day and identify prospects—people in the news, new businesses, or expanding businesses. Think about the people you are reading about—are they a direct prospect?

Or could they be a referral source? Be more creative and more assertive contacting new prospects, putting out there what you want, and need.

6. Contact your database frequently—emails, phone calls, and postcards. The last research numbers I saw said it takes 11-15 "touches" (up from 5-7 15 years ago) to get someone to talk to you and/or meet with you. Stay in front of them. One of my best projects was a prospect from 3 years ago who kept receiving my emails...and finally needed me! Don't get hung up on—"I tried 3 emails and a few phone calls, left voice messages, and they weren't interested." Your database and what you do with it keeps you in touch with people who will one day need you, when THEY need you, not when you need them!

7. Provide free, valuable content to your database. Start a newsletter, a blog, or something that will provide information to help your prospects in THEIR business. Make your contacts with them valuable to THEM, not just you.

8. Add new information to your website at least once a month.

9. Book exhibitor space at business or consumer trade shows! Give people the opportunity to see you and your products (or service) information. I invested $1200 in May 2008 (exhibit fee and travel) that has resulted in about $6000 in business so far—not a bad return—and I have all those prospects I met that still get information from me. INVEST in those expos/shows that are right for your business based on the audience and the traffic expected.

10. Attend every business expo in your area. Lots of Chambers and professional groups hold business or consumer expos during the year. If you can't exhibit because the cost is just too high for your budget right now, or it's not the right venue for you to exhibit, at least attend.

    Collect as many business cards as you can from the exhibitors who might need your products or services for their business or for themselves personally. DON'T take up their time selling yourself or your product to them—ask three quick questions about their business, write your notes on the back of their card to remind you...and move on. Wish them a great show and tell them you'll call them in two weeks after they have had time to follow up on their exhibit leads.

    Then, attend any of the speakers, breakout groups, or meals that offer another opportunity to get business cards from the people on each side of you or around the entire table. Again, you are building prospects for your database. Ask those few questions that help you qualify them and write the answers on the back of their card. DON'T sell at this event, just gather!

11. Speak at events. Get on the speaking agenda for groups throughout your area—Chamber lunches, breakfasts, Rotary, professional organizations, or affinity groups. EDUCATE in those presentations—DON'T sell. Each time, you'll get two-three people who come up afterwards and ask you to call them. Your knowledge and expertise will "sell" them! If you are shy about speaking...do #12 instead.

12. Write articles. Use the knowledge you have about your products and services to provide free, educational information. Submit those articles to local publications… they are always looking for good content. And, even if none of them print your article—send it out to your database, produce it in "slicks" that you can give out at a networking event, and add it to your website Articles page.

13. Educate yourself! Keep sharpening your skills whether its learning a new computer application, attending sales training, or studying for certification in your industry—stay current in your field and be the expert people come to when they need an answer. Give answers and help freely. People will appreciate your assistance and remember you when they need your product or service.

So… beat back that "R" word and RAMP UP your activities. ADD new services. JOIN new groups. BUILD your database, TOUCH your prospects frequently, EXHIBIT, ATTEND, or SPEAK at events around town, WRITE, MANAGE TIME, and use any slow time to EDUCATE yourself!

You don't need lots of money, but you will need to make some monetary investment—Chamber and group memberships, exhibit booth fees or attendance fees, or a new ad in a new source. But these are worthwhile and important investments. It IS true that you have to spend money to make money.

Just spend it wisely and you'll see a return. Don't miss those opportunities to be available to your market and prospects. The more you are out there, the more opportunities you have to meet those customers/clients that need you!

Connect with Sandra "Sam" Black President,
Sam Black Consulting at sam@samblack.com
for sales training and sales management,
call center training, and assessment tools.

PR Secrets to Expanding Your Reach

"…If you treat people the way they should be,
you make them what they can be."
Wolfgang van Goethe, founder of the Hope School

Success Strategies from Charlotte VM Ottley

Charlotte Ottley is an Emmy Award-winning professional who has achieved remarkable success. She specializes in working with institutions and individuals in transition.

Charming, savvy, and regal, Ms. Ottley has supported Fortune 500 businesses, primarily in the financial sector, along with world-renowned individuals in achieving success through her ability to connect with people and to connect people to opportunities.

Charlotte Ottley shares:

I'm a strategist—I build collaborations for mutually beneficial outcomes toward common goals.

I've been a therapist, an educator, a media producer, on-air talent, and a chief executive officer of multiple companies nationwide. I've been a consultant, an executive liaison to some phenomenal, historic people, and I've been a director in government. However, of all the titles I have carried over the years, my best title is Edward and Delores Merritts' daughter. Because I had, bar none, the best childhood experience that I'm holding on to even to today.

How I Help People Create Success

I help individuals and institutions get through challenges, choices, and changes during significant transitions.

Time magazine called me the "Deal Maker" because I build relationships based on trust and my capabilities to get results—I'm the common denominator.

I see the need and then match people with resources. I create an environment for people to come together for a mutually beneficial relationship, and once that happens, I usually step out and they continue.

Guidance to Businesswomen Working to Fulfill Goals with Limited Access and without Emptying Your Pockets

1. Be careful of giving too much, too soon, for too little.

2. I'm not restricting it to money—"too little" falls into many categories, including professional and personal relationships. Don't be disappointed if you aren't appreciated or are not recognized. Be clear about your value, and the value of your products or services.

3. Sometimes we are so eager to get the business that we give it away and then down the line we don't understand why people don't value us.

Be careful of over extending yourself—clients don't know when you have extended yourself beyond your capacity, nor do they need to know. In those situations, when the client has expanded their expectations beyond the original agreement, let them know immediately that there will be additional costs. You may even choose to waive them, but it is important for them to know that you extended your services to reach their goal. After the fact is too late. It will become a debate on value versus compensation.

You must ask yourself some crucial questions:

- *Can I do this?*
- *Can I deliver on what I said I could do?*
- *What will it take?*
- *Do I have time?*
- *What is my back-up plan?*
- *Can I afford the time and upfront resources required?*

Make forward-moving decisions based on your ultimate goals.

Keep emotions at bay and make solid decisions based on the value of your services.

Build Real Relationships

Many people have a wrong perception of what they believe networking to be.

They go into situations with a singular focus and turn it into business card shuffle or computer roulette. Relationship building is not going to an event and saying, "This is who I am, this is my business card, and this is what I want from you." Where is the mutual? Networking is not an end point—it isn't the last stop—it's a continuing cycle.

Access often comes from those who have helped you, as they will readily endorse you; and from those you have helped as they are grateful and will readily refer you to others. They have mutual interests in giving you a passageway to access.

Three Aspects of the Networking Cycle

1. Know who you want to access and why. You must also know what you have to offer others when unexpected opportunities are presented.

2. Once you know what you want to accomplish and who can help to obtain it, be selective in seeking networking opportunities. Choose carefully so that you can best position yourself when faced with an opportunity.

3. Once you have found a match, believe that you are worthy of it and be prepared to maximize it. Follow up and make sure that it is mutually beneficial. This is what makes opportunities multiple and the cycle of selective networking pay off.

Public Relations is the first step of any relationship.

I define it as "effectively educating one source about another source for an 'assumed' mutual gain."

One of the biggest mistakes people make in PR is failing to establish up front their expectations of each other, and then clearly stating what they have to offer for the expected outcome.
- Always start by bringing your best intentions to the table.
- Don't expect any more than what you are willing to give and

clearly outline the measurable value of your proposition.

- Too often this conversation comes too late and is built on too many assumptions.
- Get it right at first and you will have fewer misunderstandings later.

"What's in for you? What's in it for me?"

Put your "it" on the table on day one. If "it" is a concern of yours—please define "it" up front. Be honest with yourself and the other person about your expected outcome because you are going to have to live with it—whether more comes out than you ever dreamed of, or more commonly, less comes out than you expected.

If our great expectations are not met once we are in the middle of "the deal," there's no easy way back.

This is usually why people end up with bad relationships at the end: because it didn't start honestly and openly, with a clear understanding of what each can and will deliver. Each person gets to make a choice. Both must shoulder the responsibility of their commitments.

If challenges arise and you have built the relationship on trust, both parties will move quickly to alternatives for the best outcome.

Five Commitments People Must Make to Build Relationships

1. Be the best you can be at whatever you do. This will benefit you as well as others.

2. Be sincere when you approach people for assistance. Also be sincere in your response to others when they approach you for assistance. Be encouraging without giving

false hope. Don't take their requests lightly, nor your response.

3. Be proud, enthusiastic, and willing to share whatever you do. True success comes with a spirit of "let's."

4. See beyond the obstacles for the ultimate good and always remember why you are seeking the relationship. Consider alternatives, profitability, and potential outcomes before giving up or cutting your loses.

5. Give without reservation and with gratitude. Sometimes there's nothing that others can give you. The mutual benefit is not always immediate. And don't worry about reciprocity.

Nine Steps to Launching Your Public Relations Initiative

1. Know your product. Research your subject thoroughly in launching any public relations initiative. Review the background including the weaknesses, the strengths, and the expectations.

2. Develop strategies for both the strengths and the weaknesses in the pitch and positioning of your message. In other words, what is your angle, focus, or "the spin?"

3. Preparing your message is critical. The presentation of your message varies from topic to topic and the media you plan to use. You must package and appeal to the media outlet that you are using be it TV, newspaper, radio, or the Internet.

4. Develop a budget. You will have to pay for some strategies, and others you can get free through in-kind, barter, or collaborative efforts.

5. Adjust your spin (strategy and positioning) as necessary—and capitalize on unexpected opportunities that present themselves. Often your budget dictates how much you can do and for how long.

6. Monitor and track your results so that you can make critical changes to stay on course with your objectives. At some point, you will be held accountable. Be able to present your results as you go, so you are not in a position to have to defend later.

7. Throughout this process, always thank and acknowledge your sources and be sure to continue to include and inform all stakeholders.

   You always want to empower and position those who have been most helpful to you. Express your gratitude instantly to those who are responsive—by acts of gratitude like letters of thank you, and by including their contribution in your reports to others.

   I'm currently working with Michael McMillan. He is sincerely a master at giving unsolicited credit to others in everything he does.

8. Archive and chronicle your results and feedback for effective management, future development, and accountability.

9. Engage the community every step of the way. Community engagement is imperative, though many focus primarily on media.

Community Engagement is an Important Element to Your PR Success Strategy

Community engagement is a form of what is commonly referred to as "access marketing." The community is your end consumer and is the stakeholder in whatever you do. You cannot assume that your message will get to them in the way you intend unless you make efforts to reach/touch them directly.

Part of community engagement is creating strategic collaborations, joint ventures, and partnerships by finding the most likely partners to get the message out. Keep in mind that you must identify and be clear about what's important to everyone.

Another component of community engagement can be gathering decision makers who could propel your concept before you ever hit the media. This is an important stage because they can make or break the outcome if they do not truly understand the beneficial factors and endorse them.

Get Connected by Power Brokering

The "right people" vary from situation to situation, target markets, your mission, and what you are trying to accomplish. The value of power brokering is priceless. (This is why selectively building your network in line with your goals is so important).

Solicit and leverage the support of people who have the greatest to gain in what you are trying to accomplish. A room with the "right" people in it, having a shared vision, can still move mountains (which the media may likely report).

Two PR Must-Dos When Leading the Initiative

1. Build a consensus between you and your PR subject. Make sure that all parties agree with the direction that you are getting ready to go—and that each is prepared for the level of exposure and scrutiny. Remember, not all media/PR guarantees good outcomes. Avoid miscommunication through using "show and tell" examples to prevent "I thought you meant..." conversations in the future.

2. Identify the target group for your message and for the strategy that you have developed—then, determine the best method of reaching them.

Decide the exposure you really want—and then figure out how you can get it. Levels and types of exposure are different. Sometimes your message is just general information because you are building name recognition and credibility; or you may be defending or justifying something; and at other times you may be selling or motivating people to act.

Four Considerations in Selecting Professional Representation

This professional could be a publicist, agency, an agent, a manager, or a company.

1. Review their track record. Get testimonials, not just references, and find out how they were able to deliver in the past. Consider the budgets, resources, and environment in which they were able to accomplish previous results. You

can start this conversationally by simply asking questions. Past success does not guarantee that they will have the same experience with you.

2. Look beyond credentials. Make sure your resources and budget are comparable to the examples they are giving you in their record of accomplishments.

   Ask if they will be able to deliver comparable results to match your needs and your budget. For example, someone who was working with a big corporation may not be able to deliver those same results with their current resources as an independent consultant.

   Not all consultants are created equal.

   Don't be overly impressed with titles and name-dropping. Look at proof of performance and their ability to describe for you in detail what they did, why they did it, how they problem solved, and what it took to get the final outcome.

3. When you agree to fee, pay it, and pay it on time. However, always have conditions for termination understood up front. Remember there are no guarantees, only guaranteed effort. Choose a consultant who is going to give you 100% effort for whatever the two of you agree the compensation would be.

4. Identify a professional who that values you as a client. If someone views their services to you as doing you a favor, that's all it will be—and you will not be a priority. Do you want to be the big fish in the small consultant's pond

or a little fish in a big consultant's pond? They both have advantages and disadvantages. Trust your own judgment.

5.   Accountability and responsiveness are paramount. If an agent is intolerant of your inquiries, it may be a red flag, and they may not be for you so, cut your losses.

     However, once you chose an agency, trust them and let them do their job—because if you knew what they knew, you wouldn't need them.

Final Thoughts

- Don't give it, if you would not want it given to you.

- Don't accept it, if you do not believe you can handle it.

- Don't say it, if you don't believe it and know it to be true.

- Don't do it, if you are not proud of it.

- Don't fear sharing good. It will come back to you in many ways and from many sources.

Most important, when giving your best…

> *"Do not tire in well doing for you will reap the harvest of your labors in due season, if you faint not (give up)."*
> Galatians 6:9

Charlotte is an advocate for women. In 2010, The Charlotte Merritts Ottley Transitional Women's Center, founded by the Black Alcohol/ Drug Service and Information Center (BASIC) was dedicated in her name in St. Louis, Missouri.

Charlotte Ottley is featured in Donald Trump's book *The Best Business Advice I Ever Received,* and in *=Sister Strength* by Rev. Dr. Susan Johnson Cook. Charlotte is launching her first book, *Strategies to Survive Success*, available on Mission Possible Press.

Get Connected with Charlotte
at www.cottleystl.com or email
cottley@cottleystl.com to develop your personal or
professional market development strategy.

The Business of Books

"Standing in for the reader—I am the reader's representative here on earth and how it sounds to me is what I consider when I'm editing."

Publishing Wisdom from Christine Frank

What are five things people should consider when writing a book?

1. Know where, how, and to whom you will sell it first.

2. Select a form of organization to keep track of material to put in chapter by chapter. Try mind mapping software (try Evernote), on paper, on the net, but having a file for each chapter. Place thoughts and material in the specific file as they occur to you and, in a way, the book writes itself.

3. Get a team of experts—be prepared to hire a team to help you get your writing out into the world. This will include a cover designer; an editor; and book layout, marketing, and promotion experts.

4. A great cover is 50% of the battle.

Why is a good book cover so important?

It really is true that people judge a book by its cover. People can be shallow and do judge by appearances. An unprofessional cover will make even a good book unsaleable (the converse is true, too). The book cover is a great marketing tool, which you can use before the book is even written to promote it, using it in your e-mail sig or on bookmarks or business cards, for instance.

5. Try multitasking—don't just write the book—write two or three books at once; or a book and a blog; or a screenplay and a book; you are already in the throes of writing and extra material will come to you. The material sorts itself (especially if you sort it in chapters) and there is a great opportunity for multiple projects.

    If you have two, three, or four products at once, each one has a multiplier effect on the other. A book, workbook, screenplay, and TV show, for example. You can spread out the extra energy and material—you have more credibility if you've got one of *this*, and *this*, and *this*. You build a small multimedia empire and you get more bang for your buck.

What are four things people should not do when writing a book?

1. Don't try to skimp on production. For instance, using Word for layout. It's meant for word processing, not for page design.

2. Don't try to make changes once the book's laid out in the design program. You will incur extra charges and drive your designer crazy.

3. Don't envision a scene of a bookstore signing such as those you see in the movies. Non-celebrity book signings are generally useless: authors usually pay their own travel expenses, and they just don't produce sales. Approaching the casual customer is just uncomfortable, too—they are in the bookstore for something else, and you force them to reject you. Uncomfortable.

4. Don't try to use every ten-dollar word you know. Don't go crazy with adverbs. Also: "A real poet does not say *azure*. A real poet says *blue.*" (As a real poet once said.)

What is ghostwriting and why do people do it?

People often need to get a book out and don't have the time or expertise to write it themselves. So a ghostwriter, who may or may not get credit, takes over the research and writing tasks. There are all sorts of variations along the spectrum—from taking notes or interviewing and writing to wholesale fabrication of an entire work.

What are the four biggest obstacles to publishing a book?

1. Cost. People are often surprised at what they need to pay for and what it costs. Example: with both traditional and self-publishing, authors are often surprised to know that they are responsible for the index. It's just one of those quirks of the publishing industry. I mean, they don't pay for editing or postage; where's the logic?

2. You must have a platform—although this is an overused word—it's true and important. What's a platform? Your mailing list, your fans, your contacts, your clients, former students, people with whom you do business. Since we are

not relying on bookstores for sales anymore, you ought to be able to hit the ground running and send the publishing announcement to 5,000 of your closest friends. They can come from your blog, your website, other writings, and customers.

3. Trying to make the book too "special." It's like with a child: with your first one you want to do everything different and special but, books, like children, really do better in life if they resemble other similar books. The way to this is to do a "Borders Walk" where you find books in your genre—say it's a cookbook—then mimic it: make it resemble in price, dimensions, color schemes, layout, and other conventions. For instance, many wedding planning books are turquoise and square with white scripty titles. True crime books are trade paperbacks with red and black covers. Business books have simple, striking covers with titles of just a few words. Those are just a few examples.

4. Time. There are a lot of stories of people who have taken five to fifteen years to get their book out. Why? Either from perfectionism, lack of attention to tasks, or financial hurdles. I know of several instances where the authors painstakingly insisted on bartering for every service; that's noble, green, and sometimes necessary, but think of the opportunity costs of not having the book out sooner. Just get creative and pay for it somehow. I also know of some wonderful stories of creative fundraising to pay for the book.

What is the benefit of getting your book out there earlier?

It generates its own energy; it helps you to get new clients, brings in new work, opens opportunities for speaking or collaborating or writing more books. Bringing opportunities that wouldn't have been open if that book were still sitting in the computer…. Do whatever it takes, to pay if necessary, to get it out there quicker.

What are Three Things You Really Want People to Know About Books?

1. They deserve to be the best they can be. I believe the written word is sacred and should be as perfect as it can be and be in a lovely container.

2. Despite modern technology—and personally, I love most of it—books are not going away. So go ahead and start writing, put it on paper—it can always go on a Kindle later. Don't worry that books are going away.

3. I fervently believe that reading to, or sharing books with your child is a lasting gift. I was fortunate in that I had two parents who read, and who read to me. Many people today talk about bringing back the family dinner as a remedy to childhood obesity and other social ills and, as a similar concept, I see reading to children another habit that needs to be, in some cases, resurrected, and in others, introduced, for the good of our futures.

What is editing?

There are many types of editing but they all have a goal of perfecting a manuscript as it passes from author to reader. It can be as simple as fixing punctuation and capitalization or as complicated as abandoning chapters and rewriting the entire content.

Why do you do it?

It's all I've ever done, really. I started with the junior high newspaper. I attended North Kirkwood Jr. High and I have often said that everything I learned was from the journalism teacher there. Though that can't be true because I've read many miles of books and had lots of formal schooling since then.

What is indexing?

Indexing produces a tool located at the back of a non-fiction book to help the reader find specific topics—the index. It is distinct from a concordance, which confuses a lot of people. A concordance can be generated automatically by software but an index is a specific, cerebral, painstaking, editorial task. Sometimes I read a book three times, and have three or four drafts of an index. It's a work of art in itself.

What is your life's purpose?

It can't be about fixing commas—can it? I would like to think that it is about making life easier for animals—protecting and saving animals. Except for one cat at a time, I'm not really there yet.

How long have you been in business?

Well, I got my first business license in 1997. Before that, I had corporate jobs in editing.

I had been working toward my own business, I lived in Virginia Beach at the time, and there wasn't much opportunity for corporate work. You were either a sailor or worked for the railroad. So I had a shiny new master's in writing degree, the Internet had just taken off, and it became possible for me to go out on my own, at that time.

How do you get most of your business?

Referrals or from other vendors: designers, illustrators, printers, and publishers, for instance, who send people to me.

Do you still read for pleasure?

Oh yes!

One of my end-of-the-year rituals is to go through the *New York Times* Books of the Year list and reserve the ones that look good at the library. So this way I get a constant stream of new books.

It's not just about saving money, but a storage problem. I buy non-fiction—about design, book production, or self-help—but fiction, I can't keep in the house because I usually only read it once, and it collects dust then I have to move it. Though I do keep a few. For instance, George Orwell will always have a place on my bookshelves.

What services do you provide?

Book coaching, editing, ghost writing, project management for books, and indexing.

I like dealing with associations, organizations, and institutions, and individuals writing books to promote their business. A goal is that I would like to do work for foundations or think tanks. I would like to split my time between living in St. Louis and Washington, DC.

What are your goals for the future?

Besides what I've already mentioned—working for a think tank in DC? And saving animals? I would love for one of my authors to become a major success, and soon I will be ready for another ghostwriting project. I wouldn't mind living in Europe again, either.

If you have written or are writing a book and don't know how to get it into print, contact Christine. She provides the services needed to take it from a manuscript to the printer's door.

Get Connected to Christine Frank and Associates at
www.christinefrank.com.

Section Three
The Acceleration

Connecting and Relating

Establish Your Name and Reputation

"A Good name is more desired than great riches;
to be esteemed is better than silver or gold."
Proverbs 22:1(NIV)

Communication Insights from Jo Lena

Professional Recommendations and Business References are Crucial to Your Growth

Recommendations and references make a huge impact on building your business because character, integrity, and preparedness make a difference. It was because of "investing" in a 7 AM BNI (Business Networking International) weekly meeting that I first learned of Donna Gamache.

One morning, BNI Member Bart Ratliff recommended to the group that we participate in an upcoming fundraiser. What I heard him say was that I could gain business exposure, potentially gain new customers, support a good cause, and interact with women business owners in St. Louis, all by spending $100 to become a sponsor for an eWomenNetwork Foundation fundraising event. The words he chose and the confidence he showed, coupled with the fact that he has a long-standing relationship with eWomenNetwork as a sponsor, influenced me to take action.

You see, Bart's business is SendOutCards (www.SendOutCards.com/bart). His enthusiasm, confidence, and high energy, coupled with experience make him well suited for that business and he is highly successful in it. After the meeting, I did some research about the eWomenNetwork and was so impressed at what I read that I was excited to catch up with Donna Gamache. I felt by participating I was making a sound investment in my business, in expanding my circle, and in my fun too, since it was a "trivia night" event.

Bart had given Donna and eWomenNetwork one of the strongest business endorsements I had ever heard. One of the best things you can do for yourself is learn, read (you have a great start, with this book!), and ask people who have achieved success in similar endeavors. When choosing with whom to invest your time, energy, and resources, one of the best ways to start is with a trusted source and by doing your own research. Many organizations, groups, and people are willing to support you—if you are willing to find them and to listen.

Practice Good People Skills

*"Do not withhold good from those who deserve
it, when it is in your power to act. "*
Proverbs 3:27(NIV)

Communication Insights from Jo Lena

Show People You Care—Good People Skills Require Flexibility

In her own words, Donna describes herself as "warm and friendly, a good listener, and as 'a connector'." I hadn't heard that term before so, she explained, "I'm good at bringing people together for business, friendship, and/or synergy." I smiled when she said that because it's true, she does!

I met Donna at the fundraiser. During the evening I noticed how she coordinated the volunteers; gave input about the silent auction; was an enthusiastic mistress of ceremonies; and how she visited each participant table, sponsor table, connecting, having fun, and listening to people—all while keeping a warm smile on her face.

The night we met, Donna had a full plate. She was focused on raising funds for the foundation; she was delightful; she cheered the trivia game winners; she comforted (us) non-winners; she wished everyone safe passage while praising people for investing their time, talent, and resources; and she remained time conscious—it was time to vacate the premises! *Wouldn't it be great if all business meetings went that well?*

Acknowledging people's participation is simply good practice, and essential to building good relationships. What Donna "showed me" was that she was creative, efficient, had a good sense of time; had done an excellent job of recruiting people to the event; and that she really cared about giving. By closing the evening with rounds of genuine "thank yous," Donna showed me that she knows how to treat people well. And people want to be treated well when in relationships.

Create Valuable Relationships

Jo Lena and Donna Chat

"Building a relationship with another person—not just to do business the first few times—but really getting to know, them is vitally important."
Donna Gamache

Connecting Starts with Finding out What the Other Person Really Needs

Jo Lena: As a connector, you meet and interact with quite a few women every week. Is there a common thread you see in what women are attempting to accomplish with their businesses?

Donna: Yes, women want to make the right connections for business. They want to sell their products and services, and need ways to get in front of potential clients.

Jo Lena: What do you tell them, and what can you recommend to our readers?

Donna: Of course, I tell them about eWomenNetwork and resources we offer women through our website and at local events. Then, I let them know that making connections is not just about telling someone about your products and services. It truly is about finding out how you can help the other person first.

When meeting someone for the first time, ask, "How can I help you today?" I learned this from the founder of eWomenNetwork, Sandra Yancey. Not only does this set you apart from everyone else trying to push their information, it give you the satisfaction of knowing you helped.

In my personal interactions while out networking, I ask people what they need and they typically ask what I need too. When both parties know what they really want, and can share it clearly, concisely, and really listen to the other party as well, this sets the foundation for a strong relationship built on caring and giving.

If you are like me, you will need to make notes (mental or written) about what they need help with. The one piece that is missing for so many is the follow-up. So, make sure you take those notes and follow up. For me, sending an email introduction is the quickest way to help them. Scheduling a follow-up coffee to gather more information is important in connecting them with the right resource. Whatever method you use, just make sure you take the time to follow up!

Connecting Continues with Knowing What You Really Want

Jo Lena: Once you have asked about what they need and followed up, then what happens as you connect with the other person?

Donna: I meet many women who really don't know what they want. Or, at least they don't know how to verbalize what they want. I suggest taking time to center in on and focus on your priorities.

If you need help with this, find a coach who can help you. They can help you put together an effective and short sentence that lets others know what you want.

Notice I said short sentence. It needs to be short so people really listen. Face it, when you ramble on and on you lose their attention.

"Who is your perfect client?"

You need to know who your perfect client is, so make a list of the qualities your ideal client would have, getting down to details like industry, function, services provided, size of firm, personality styles, work style preferences, and even down to the way you'd like to communicate. If you are comfortable working with people virtually, for example, or if you would prefer face-to-face contact when working with them. By being able to identify your perfect client you can tell others who you need to connect with for business.

Once you've told me specifically who you are looking for, then people, organizations, or resources will pop into my head. I usually follow up with an email introduction connecting the right persons.

How Do I Meet Potential Clients, Get More Business, and Market Myself?

Donna Answers

These are my top three questions asked by entrepreneurs.

#1. How do I meet potential clients?

You won't meet the right clients sitting in your office working on your task list. It is so easy for us as sole entrepreneurs to spend hours a day working in our business, especially for those of us who work in our homes. I can spend hours upon hours answering emails, sending emails, and doing busy work that keeps me from doing what I really need to do: getting out and meeting people.

It reminds me of being single and asking how to meet a man when all I do is sit at home. How do you expect to meet potential clients if you are not out networking? Do you think they will knock on your door? That typically does not happen when one is single. At least, it sure didn't happen to me.

The way to meet potential clients is to get out of your office.

Sure, you can meet potential clients on the Internet. Social media has really made that more of a possibility, but it will never take the place of relationship networking. Those you meet in person are more likely to become clients and stay clients.

#2. How do I get more business?

It truly is a numbers game. The more people you have in your personal network, the more chances you have for selling your products and services. I'm not telling you something you don't already know. Yet, I talk to so many new business owners who don't have a very robust network. Just as I mentioned earlier, you have to get out and network at least one time a week to build your database of contacts.

Then take time to build a relationship with those in your network. I'm not talking about taking them out for coffee every week, but I am talking about having some point of contact on a regular basis. Maybe it's a phone call, a newsletter, a blog, or a card. Something that keeps their focus on what you have to offer.

Just think about your own experience. You go to a networking event and you meet someone with a product or service you are interested in buying. As soon as you leave that event, your mind starts to shift to everything you need to get done and you forget about that great product or service. It happens to all of us. That's why it is so important to create a system for keeping in touch with them. Out of sight, out of mind, so keep in touch.

And, exposure is equally as important. Look for ways to display your products and/or marketing materials. At eWomenNetwork, you can purchase a table to sell at the event. Think of other ways to keep your offerings in front of your potential clients.

#3. *How do I market myself?*

First, make sure your brand is polished and concise. Remember, you are your brand and you are marketing yourself everywhere you go. Here are some things I've learned over the last 10 years of being a business owner.

Join a group that will provide you opportunities to tell who you are and what you do. Of course, I recommend eWomenNetwork because that is exactly what you get to do at the events. Joining a group is a personal choice, and the important thing is to be a part of a group that offers opportunities for you-to promote yourself and your offerings.

When you join your group of choice, make sure you show up and get actively involved. If you are shy, I suggest you start with a woman's group that teaches you to do a 60-second introduction. Find a more seasoned networker and go with her to see how they meet new people.

Be genuine and sincere when you ask, "How can I help you?" People will remember you as someone who cares.

Be professional in your dress and in your business materials. You only have 3 seconds to make a first impression, so make sure you look your best and have a professional business card and materials to leave behind.

Defining Conflict and Overcoming Fear

"If fear becomes bigger than faith, you are keeping success at bay."

Insight from Jo Lena

If you understand, you have the ability to apply.

The number one cause of conflict is lack of (or) mis-communication. The primary cause of conflict, which is the lack of communication or miscommunication, is typically rooted in cultural differences.

Culture can include society, education, geographic territory, race, socio-economic class, or other factors. Yet, day to day, conflict between people most often happens for one of three reasons or all three reasons: gender differences, generational differences, or personality style differences.

When you are attempting to accomplish a goal, it's important to know where you are going, why you are going, what tools you need, and how to actually use them, lest you forget the intended destination itself.

Every day there are "opportunities" for conflict. Sometimes our conflicts are external, things like natural disasters, or they are internal like poor self-esteem or previous negative experiences. Still, at other times they can be managed by your own willingness to learn, grow, stretch, and try different ways of thinking, acting, or behaving.

Success isn't just about a big contract, luxury, or fancy titles; it's also about quality of life, energy, and harmony in the areas that are important to you, as an individual and as a business owner.

The poem by Marianne Williamson, titled, "Our Deepest Fear," addresses overcoming conflict...

"Our Deepest Fear"
Our deepest fear is not that we are inadequate.
Our deepest fear is that we are powerful beyond measure.
It is our light, not our darkness that most frightens us.
We ask ourselves,
Who am I to be brilliant, gorgeous, talented, and fabulous?
Actually, who are you not to be?
You are a child of God.
Your playing small does not serve the world.
There is nothing enlightened about shrinking so that other people
won't feel insecure around you.
We are all meant to shine, as children do.
We were born to make manifest the glory of God that is within us.
It is not just in some of us; it is in everyone.
And as we let our own light shine, we unconsciously
give other people permission to do the same.
As we are liberated from our own fear,
our presence automatically liberates others.

[Excerpt from Marianne Williamson's book, "A Return To Love: Reflections on the Principles of A Course in Miracles," published by Harper Collins.]

Your connectedness and your success are your own. If you really want to experience it, you must find what liberates you and begin to embrace it.

How "Life" Impacts You

You learned a lot about life based on the behavior of your parents, your elders, your peers, your neighborhood, and other generational influences. Some things are easily modified and others, not so much.

Choose to focus on what's most important to you. The result? *What you really want*—by knowing what you don't want!

Many women who have shared in this book have found the connections they needed to overcome conflict, achieve their goals, and to make a difference in every life they touch. You, too, have that ability!

When faced with opportunities for conflict, I recommend that you face it—directly—and figure out how to overcome it. Use your internal and external resources so that you can be objective and get perspective before making any rash or emotional decisions.

Overcoming Conflict is Not Easy

During the writing of this book, Donna and I were busy and we found it difficult to connect. Donna loves to get together—she communicates most effectively in person because she's a connector and a visual learner. On the other hand, for lack of time because of my travel schedule, focused attention on writing, training, and managing my business while trying to complete these book projects, I really wanted to talk on the phone or email.

We had tried emailing. However, when you write things down, you are only communicating a portion of your message—and that can lead to misinterpretation of tone. That's important to know because if you are not "connected" to those with whom you work and play, it's easy to have a miscommunication (conflict) with someone and not even know it—because the other party may not share their thoughts or feelings in a way that you understand, appreciate, or agree with.

In the case of Donna and me as co-authors, during the final editing of this book, for example, Donna emailed and said, "I'm not sure if I agree with everything that the interviewees or you said." To that I replied, "It's not up to us to agree or disagree with a contributor's aspirations because we are including these stories and such to give perspective and choice to our readers."

In the early stages of writing this book, we had agreed that if there was something which might be misconstrued, we would pick up the phone—at the very least—and get through whatever the concerns might be. So when this email communication happened, we both "got into action."

Instead of taking a "stand," since we both have strong personalities, I called my father, Kenneth Johnson, and asked him to give me his perspective. He listened and then said, "Writing a book with another person is like being married…" Whew, he was right. By simply connecting with him, and being willing to listen to his wisdom and guidance, it helped me to be open to working through a mutually agreeable solution.

Unbeknownst to me, Donna did the same thing. She reached out and connected with several trusted, objective confidantes who assisted her in looking at the situation slightly differently. When we addressed the issue again, we solved it. And, this "opportunity for conflict" gave us both the chance to grow, and to add this section to the book.

We agree that it's okay to disagree but not okay to stop working through each person's concerns—and that's the beauty of wisdom and experience.

There's no drama behind our "story;" we all have experience and much to gain by listening, considering, and communicating. Being truly successful is about coming through—and I'm glad for the lessons, growth, and experiences that daily shape me as a professional and entrepreneur.

Here's my favorite mantra—if you need it, you can use it too: "I'm a gentle servant in progress." It may not always feel like it, but it's something to continually aspire to!

Identify What You Do Well!

"Becoming skilled takes practice, practice, practice"
Jo Lena Johnson

Do you know your top five skills?

If you do, great! If you don't, get to work!

As you continue reading, notice that each of the women interviewed for this book is self-aware and freely acknowledges what works (for her), and at times, what hasn't worked. Though each individual is unique, you will notice some common, effective trends that work—if practiced.

It's really important for you to know what you do well, and be able to identify "opportunities for growth." As a business owner, it's easy to try to do everything. It takes courage to admit what you don't know or areas that need some work. People who work with you will appreciate it too.

Confidence is very attractive and even magnetic. Too many women don't consider themselves "leaders" or attain the success they deserve because they haven't taken the time to do some simple, honest assessment.

Donna Shares Her Top Five Skills

1.   Creating a harmonic lifestyle. Growing your business should include your personal and professional needs, goals, and roles.

2.   Managing people. People can include your partners, children, friends, and those who actually work with and for you.

3.   Computer literacy. Local libraries usually offer free courses in small time blocks to teach basic programs for no charge.

4.   Being a good speaker/presenter. Knowing what you want to say, in a way that people understand, takes preparation and practice.

      a.   Watch what others do/don't do well.

      b.   Participate in good training courses. They will help you.

      c.   Stand in front of your mirror and practice your presentation (including your winning smile!)

5.   Productivity. Through using daily task lists, time blocking, and making allowances for spontaneity and fun, you allow yourself the freedom to complete projects and to be successful in your whole life—professionally and personally.

Your opportunity while reading is to "find the learning" that you can store in your own wellspring of knowledge. If you don't know, this is a great time to acknowledge what you do well.

What are your top five skills?

Make Your Image Count,
With and Without Your Presence

Donna Recommends

*"If people do not understand what it is you do, they
will not know why they need your services."*

Branding with Collateral Materials and Attire Builds
Confidence for You, and In You

a. **Your Electronic Image**—Purchasing a personalized domain email
address increases your credibility, shows you are serious about your
business, and is a great investment. Consider your email address:
for less than $13 per month you can get numerous email addresses
through entities like Godaddy.com or through Yahoo!™Small
Business—which typically includes website options. Even if you're
not ready for a website, going this route is still one of the best
branding decisions you can make.

b. **Introductions**—Oftentimes women share way too much
information. People may not understand the function and value of
your business. Creating a concise introduction enhances your efforts
in every way.

c. **A One-Sheet**—Every business woman should have one. It is simple, concise, and explains what products or services you offer and how people can contact you. If people do not understand what it is you do, they will not know why they need your services.

d. **Attire**—A woman doesn't have to be dressed in a designer outfit to look professional—but she does need to dress to fit her own personal style. When a woman knows her own style, she is more confident and positioned to make a great first impression.

If affordability is important to you, visit a second-hand store or boutique and find a jacket that fits your style personality but maybe not your body shape. Taking that jacket to a tailor and having it fitted to your body shape makes it looks like you've spent a lot of money on it.

You may be thinking, "Why a jacket?" The reason I say jacket is because that's what usually gets most people's attention. You can buy pants, tops, and accessories at discount stores, paying a lot less money than you would buying them in specialty stores.

Project your style personality through accessories. It may be a beautiful scarf that draws attention to your face and to your beautiful smile. For some, it may be about the right piece of jewelry. For others, it's all about the shoes.

Look like you are serious about handling your business.

It is so important for a woman in business to look like a woman in business. When you go out you never know who you are going to run into! The details matter and some of your best clients will come and stay because they appreciate and value your business "presentation."

Keeping Your Personal Life and Career in Harmony

Donna Shares

1. I take time every morning to have a devotional reading and to journal my appreciation and intentions.

2. I schedule my exercise at least three-four times a week. There is nothing better than exercise to relieve stress and increase energy. Notice I said schedule, because if you don't put it on your calendar and treat it like an appointment it is easier to skip it.

3. I make time for fun with my husband, family, and friends. Some of my favorite things to do are entertaining, shopping, wine tasting, and laughing.

Self-care

Self-care includes cultivating your mind, body, soul, spirit, and even your style! Since I have already talked about what you can do for your mind and spirit, let me give you some food for thought about your body.

Think about your relationship with your own body. A woman once told me she didn't like her legs because people used to tease her about them in elementary school. Now, this woman had great legs but had been wearing pants for most of her life because of something said by an elementary-aged child.

Why do we internalize these comments? We need to concentrate on the things we like about our bodies, and not get caught up in what other people say. I could really get on my soapbox about how we let the images we see in magazines, movies, and on TV affect the way we feel about our bodies. We are all created uniquely and there is beauty in all of us. So, stop letting others influence how you feel about your body and push past some of those outdated feelings.

We are each unique, unrepeatable persons, and we have so much to offer others.

Our arms are our "love handles." They are strong enough to push you up if you slip and long enough to give a hug you when you or someone else needs one!

Our legs are our "transportation." They are sturdy enough to make an about-face if you find yourself in need of retreat and they are strong enough to carry you where you really want to go!

Remain Inspired

Focus and self-care also has to do with inspiration. Sometimes a few inspirational sayings or quotes are just enough to get over an immediate hurdle.

Putting the *Source* in Human Resources

*"Ask questions when you think you have been thrown
into the fire—in a non-threatening way."*

Wisdom from Vera Spencer Johnson

Vera Spencer Johnson is a successful human resources executive in a predominately male environment. She credits her longevity and peace of mind to a few things that she thinks and does regularly, and she was kind enough to share them with us:

Vera Johnson's Action Items List
- Keep God in everything—pray before making decisions; ask for double wisdom and discernment
- Ask for favor in all things and claim the victory
- Share your faith
- Pray for others
- Learn from mistakes and always treat others with respect
- Be persistent if you believe in what you are doing

Vera's Johnson's Things to Do List
- Laugh out loud
- Enjoy your free time
- Listen more than you speak
- Ask questions when you think you have been thrown into the fire—in a non-threatening way
- Learn from old people—they have something to share

- Learn from kids—their simple views of life is profound—and it has taught me how to handle adults
- Get to know co-workers on a social basis

Six Ways to Stay Out of the Doctor's Office

"Acupuncture heals."

Wisdom from Afua Bromley L.Ac

1. Get enough sleep.
2. Stretch and exercise regularly—with a big emphasis on stretching.
3. Take time to reflect; whether it is meditating or praying, people need to reflect.
4. Have at least 60% of what you eat be vegetables and fruit (at a minimum).
5. Drink at least 64 ounces of water a day (for an adult).
6. Give or get a hug at least once a day.

Why this list?

For the most part, it covers many mental health issues. Following this regimen helps to deal with stress and manage mental health issues such as depression. I see a lot of both.

I had a patient who was complaining of knee problems, among other issues, and I recommended that she practically eliminate both salt AND sugar from her diet I recommended eliminating salt because she was retaining fluids, and sugar because it tends to have an inflammatory effect on the body, especially with joints.

I also recommended that she stop drinking all of the caffeinated diet soda that she was using to stay awake instead of sleeping.

Reasons to Eliminate Certain Drinks (and "diet" foods):

1. Carbonated beverages: Any time you are drinking them, it's tough on the kidneys. You usually run an increased chance of developing kidney stones because of the mineral content. So even when drinking seltzer water with no calories, it's harder for the kidneys to process.

2. "The Diet Part": In any kind of diet products, there is the whole element of chemical additives. Some of the artificial sweeteners, like saccharine, are known to increase your cancer risk. Others are reported to increase the risk of developing autoimmune diseases and memory issues—with an increased risk of developing Alzheimer's and dementia.

    And, though some of those studies are controversial, I don't think it's worth taking the chance.

There are more recent studies showing that, generally speaking, people who drink diet sodas are usually still shown to remain overweight. They actually think there is some evidence that the body doesn't process the artificial sweetener like a non-calorie. You don't usually see a whole bunch of people who are overweight lose weight by drinking them…and people who are thin and drink them usually stay thin.

What about the process of acupuncture?

- It doesn't hurt, most of the time. You can fit five acupuncture needles into a syringe, and techniques do vary from one practitioner to another.
- Drinking water creates a better environment and a more relaxing experience. When you are dehydrated, the needles don't go smoothly into the skin—there is more resistance in the muscle and in the skin.

- If you are afraid of needles, go in and ask the acupuncturist to do just one needle. After you get one, you will probably say, "Wow! That's it?" and then you will be ready for a full treatment. It doesn't hurt, and, after the first one needle, sometimes you don't even know that more are being placed.

Is acupuncture expensive?

It's not costly. It is sometimes covered by insurance, so it behooves you to find out. If you go into someone's private practice, office visits will vary anywhere from $45 to $95. But if that is out of your price range, there are other options:

1. Go to an acupuncture school where a student who is supervised by a licensed practitioner will see you. Those visits are usually $25.

2. Go to a community acupuncture clinic, which often runs on sliding scales. There the treatment can cost from $15 to $20, up to about $45. Some of the other services I offer are quite helpful to people—and I really enjoy teaching them how to take care of themselves.

What's the big project in Ghana you are building?

I am the director of a non-profit that has an HIV women's support group, along with HIV prevention in St. Louis. I'm also helping to build an integrative medicine non-profit clinic in Ghana, West Africa.

Why is this clinic so important?

It is a pilot/model which will hopefully be reproduced worldwide... the idea is that integrative medicine can address the various health care needs of different people. It has a strong emphasis on training public health care workers above and beyond the norms.

What does integrative medicine mean?

Integrative medicine means a wide variety of different modalities (health care practices), and we are attempting to provide them for our project in Ghana. They include:
   a. Acupuncture
   b. Traditional herbal, local medicines
   c. Counseling
   d. A "Western medicine MD"
   e. A Midwife
   f. Possibly a homeopath or another health care field

Wow, how do you find the time to do this?

I'm a workaholic.

We have the land and a water source, and we are in the process of building the facility. In terms of health care in Ghana, in the semirural areas, there is limited access. Nationally, in Ghana there is one health care provider per 10,000 people, so access is an issue.

Get Connected with Afua about the
project in Ghana, or to support it, please
visit Universalhealth.net. For acupuncture
inquiries or to schedule an appointment please
visit www.acupuncturestlouis.com.

Acknowledging Priorities

Jo Lena and Donna Chat

*"God created us, in my opinion, to have communion
with Him first, and then to work, rest, and play."*
Donna Gamache

Work, Focus, and Rest?

Jo Lena: You seem to be so flexible and far less "high strung" than me, even when you are juggling many projects. Is this natural for you or have you had to work through it?

Donna: I find that when I am too focused on one thing, I actually lose my focus all together. God created us, in my opinion, to have communion with Him first, and then to work, rest. and play.

Jo Lena: I'm glad you said that: "too focused" creates "no focus." Please share more.

Donna: If we are so focused on work and don't get the sleep we need, take time to meditate, and give thanks we could wind up spinning and spinning in a circle, thinking we are being focused on our business, yet, in reality we can't truly be focused on anything. Did you know that some of our most creative thinkers took time to play every day? Think about it: how creative can you be if you do nothing but work?

Jo Lena: I agree. While I was conducting training sessions, for several years it was five cities a week, and I didn't fully appreciate the huge toll that working so much had taken on me. It had made me more than dull—it had also worn me out, tapped my energy, and had caused a drought in my spiritual storehouse.

I would use every ounce of energy to "be available" for the participants in my classes; many times I ignored the mornings when I was losing my voice from overuse and the entire year I had to put cotton in my ears because any air caused instant headaches. My "work" needed me and I was focused.

Donna: When we are experiencing tunnel vision, we think we are being productive but it's really not possible. We are complex creatures and we need it all: communion, work, rest, and play.

Jo Lena: There are many women, and I must include myself, that know that if we aren't "producing," the bills don't get paid, the checks don't get cut for salaries, and everything, literally everything, is riding on our individual efforts. It's normal to work through meal times and play times and the computer is usually within arm's length.

Donna: That's true. For those of us who work in our homes, do you set work-time boundaries? It is so very important to set work hours, especially if you work from a home office. Even if it means shutting the door to your home office and putting a sign on the door saying "Remember, you are closed right now." Taking time to read, to relax, to sleep, and to be with girlfriends is crucial to living in harmony.

Jo Lena: I love the idea of putting a sign on the door. I think I need one on my computer as well!

Interns and Virtual Assistants
Ease the Pressure

Donna and Jo Lena Chat

Jo Lena: As an entrepreneur, the pressure to complete projects can be tremendous. What would you really like women to know about being getting affordable assistance?

Donna: Avoid taking on too much.

If you are a new business owner, it's kind of a two-edged sword because there is so much to do and you may be your only employee. You may lack the resources needed to hire the help you really need.

Look for interns who can help you with paperwork, phone calls, and such.

I had an intern working with me each week and her help was invaluable. Through the internship program, I was able to share my wisdom and experience with this young woman and in turn, she got real-world experience from me.

Most colleges and universities have intern programs. You can find out about their programs by going to their websites and visiting their career centers. The process is much easier than you might think.

Ask the intern what she or he is looking for from their experience of working with you. For me, it took several interviews to find the right fit. I needed someone who was more focused on real-world experience than payment. Alternatively, you may find someone that needs college credits versus payment or certain experiences.

To those of you who are beyond your first few years of business ownership...

If you are still trying to do it all, just stop and hire someone to help you. How can you effectively do it all? I hired an assistant and it is has been crucial to the growth of my business and believe me, once you hire an assistant it will significantly contribute to your success as well.

You are your brand. No one can represent your company as well as you can so you need to be the one networking and meeting with clients. Let someone else take care of your paperwork. And, if you don't have an office, there are many great virtual assistants that can help you as well.

Julie Eddy with Golden Services and Jeannine Clontz with Accurate Business Services are two virtual assistants in St. Louis and they are amazing.

Jo Lena: Great advice, Donna. Because I travel so much, having an intern hasn't really been an option for me. However, my friend Nicole Cleveland, the founder and publisher of *Breathe Again Magazine,* was the first to recommend a virtual assistant to me.

I was having a lot of trouble keeping up with all of my teaching responsibilities, and wasn't able to maintain connections with people as regularly as I really wanted.

When Nicole explained that the way she is able to produce her magazine, care for her family, and maintain her other relationships was with the help of a virtual assistant, I was encouraged because since it worked for her, I figured it would probably work for me.

Then, I remember feeling overwhelmed at the prospect of finding a reliable person because in the past I've had challenges with "virtual contractors" whom I had hired to build websites and things. Nicole assured me that I could find the "right person" and she helped me by sending out a Tweet.

Nicole used her Twitter connections and told her "people" that "Jo Lena Johnson needs a virtual assistant" and to contact me if anyone was interested.

Donna: Were you even on Twitter at the time? I remember you being so busy and unsure if you could commit to becoming a Tweeter.

Jo Lena: Ha, ha! You know me so well. Yes, I was already on Twitter! Nicole is the same friend that had recommended that I join Twitter, LinkedIn, and start a blog. (All excellent ways to build, reconnect, and maintain relationships.) That's one of the reasons I was feeling overwhelmed. I felt like I had these great tools available for expanding my business in the direction I wanted to go but I didn't know "how" to manage the tools and my schedule in a way that wouldn't create more work for myself.

Donna: So what did you do?

Jo Lena: I did get a couple of responses from Twitter and after screening, they weren't the right matches for me. However, Nicole also recommended the woman who had been working with her,

Corrie Petersen, owner of **Virtual Freedom 4 You**. I ended up choosing Corrie and it made a huge difference for me.

It also took a little time to incorporate her into my work style, to maximize her skills and expertise, and for me to *learn how to allow her to really help take the load off my plate.*

Donna: That's a good point—learning how to take the load off your plate is not easy. You've had many people working with and for you at one time. Do you have challenges delegating?

Jo Lena: That's a great way to put it. Yes, I, like most people, do have challenges delegating. It takes time and organization, along with a willingness to let go and trust that the work will be done, with a great result, and on time.

I have had as many as 50 contractors working with me at one time and when we were focused on marketing, promotion, and events, I was much more comfortable delegating because we had worked together, side by side, and I had trained them in the areas for which they would be responsible.

However, "trusting" someone with representing me in my stead—someone I had never met in person—wasn't an easy transition. By connecting with Nicole to get to Corrie, it eased my mind and helped me with the trust factor. Knowing what you want and need is extremely important. Juggling transactions, doing high-quality work, and wading through hectic schedules is the fabric of my life and I really needed someone who could handle that, and me.

Donna: So how did you work through the "getting started" process with your virtual assistant?

Jo Lena: In preparation for working together, I asked Corrie the question, "How I can be most effective in using your services?" That conversation was particularly helpful in starting a successful connection for us. I highly recommend asking that question because it can save all business owners time and potential miscommunication.

Gain Time and Freedom with Virtual Assistance

"What I do helps people grow their businesses."

Insight from Corrie Petersen

Why did you create your virtual assistant enterprise?

Corrie Petersen shares:

I love to help people. What I do helps people grow their businesses. I feel a sense of accomplishment. The lifestyle. I love computers, being on the Internet, and it's great for me to do business completely online.

Six Really Good Reasons to Work with a Virtual Assistant

1. As a business owner, you may want to grow and expand your business but you don't have enough time and need to outsource certain things.

2. There may be things you know that you need to do but you may not know how to do them. I can assist you!

    Submitting articles to publications is a great example of how you can gain exposure, build your business, and educate potential new customers. Once you've written the articles

I can submit them to entities within your target market. Too many documents of all kinds are collecting "cyber dust" because they haven't been circulated.

3. Perhaps your team has grown and you may struggle with remaining connected and staying in touch regularly. If I can submit articles, create newsletters, and complete other tasks that will help with the communication process, you can build bridges, and have more time to focus on your team.

4. Having assistance can help to give you more time in to spend with your family.

5. I can collaborate with you to make things bigger and better. This works because we put our minds together to brainstorm and come up with things you may not have come up with on your own.

6. I can help keep you organized.

Because I care for my clients, I do the best job every time. I have excellent customer service skills and I'm here for the duration—I'm not going anywhere.

Corrie Petersen is the owner of Virtual Freedom 4 You, a virtual assistant business that she founded in early 2006. She enjoys helping others spend more time with their families while growing their businesses. She helps her clients with affiliate programs, blogs, article marketing, and more.

Get Connected with Corrie
and see how she can help you grow at
http://www.virtualfreedom4you.com.

Section Four
The Tools

Resources and Tips

Mastering Learning Curves and Managing Expectations

"Communicating effectively takes practice, practice, practice!"

Insight from Jo Lena Johnson

"Managing" your clients is not an easy task, and is often necessary if you are going to provide the products and services they *really* need. When you are attempting to support people in growth and development, it's tough because most of us *don't really want* to change. In order for you to be truly successful, you must be willing to risk, lead, and facilitate results to produce the desired outcome while gently pushing and pulling everyone involved along the way.

Sometimes people get excited when they hear that I conduct training sessions and that I am also known as a public speaker. For some reason, many people think it's glamorous and "fun" to stand in front of people and talk. What I say is that it's hard work and can be considerably rewarding. I don't look at it as "talking," though, because it is a tremendous honor and responsibility to share time with people and help them with their needs.

In another book, I'll go into detail about specific ways to be an effective trainer, speaker, or facilitator; however, right now, what I'd really like you to know is that building your business takes hard work and experience. I didn't start off one day and say, "I think I want people to sit and listen to me all day…"

Communicating effectively takes effort and patience.

I learned that before I started "teaching people" how to lead and communicate in formal training settings.

In 1998, I founded Absolute Good as a marketing and promotion company and I overcame communication challenges because I was willing to work through challenges, and in order to stay in business.

I hired and trained an event field staff which grew to 50 in four years. I noticed that many, including one of my primary clients, often had unrealistic expectations about what it takes to grow or develop projects and people. That plans and tasks, organization and structure, and research are great—and then there is the business of people.

Individuals had needs, unique experiences, and perspectives, which were being ignored. I learned to overcome conflict by communicating effectively—and I was building relationships in the process—even when it was challenging.

My Role: *I managed the West Coast marketing and field efforts (on site promotions) for my client, who was located on East Coast.*

My Accomplishments: *A 300% increase in sales; gained exclusive access to targeted trendsetters and celebrities; and established a production, execution, and training model for future efforts.*

My Responsibilities:

Scheduling, organizing, and managing people, staff, external vendors, and my client!

Hard work, establishing a team of willing people, and building relationships.

What it took From Me:

1. **Respect and Responsibility:** Using clients' time and budgetary guidelines, along with creative activities and knowledge of each unique market.

2. **Results**: My market was 50% larger than that of my six counterparts in other areas of the U.S. We were about three times as successful, because I had two separate markets, and went beyond the "blueprints" that my clients had laid out.

3. **Planning:** Creating a new system and then tactfully educating the client to use the system in order to effect change.

4. **Energy, Enthusiasm, Passion, and Frequent Flyer Benefits:** To deliver desired results of the client and to manage challenging circumstances, different expectations, schedules, and familiarity with airports

5. **Courage to Share Opportunities for Growth and Development:** Instead of "making anyone wrong," I communicated in ways that made clear the distinctions between what was working or not, and shared in terms that were important and meaningful to them.

The Results:

I simultaneously created and managed relationships with three radio stations, three wholesale distributors, 84 retail vendors, nine major record labels, 22 event promoters, and countless customers.

During first 3 months, I created, produced, and executed two simultaneous campaigns in Northern and Southern California, resulting in 62 retail events, 184 new product case sales, four partnerships with local promoters, my Absolute Good staff increase, and the training of 18 people. I produced 300+ events in 3 years, internal and external staff training quarterly, and travel two or three times weekly.

Seven Action Steps to Getting and Staying Connected with the Inner You

"Manage through the past and focus on this moment."

Leadership Strategy from Jo Lena Johnson

1. **Make** your spiritual connection your number one priority; you will be grateful for the strength and fortitude in times of difficulty and in times of peace.
2. **Show** the posture of a servant; turn humility and confidence into tenacity, especially when times are tough.
3. **Forgive** yourself and others; no one is perfect, and especially not you!
4. **Build and maintain** relationships with people who look like you and who don't look like you; it's critical to your success.
5. **Be willing to let go** of those situations, circumstances, and people who no longer deserve you.
6. **Be willing to admit** …when you don't know, when you need to know, and when you don't understand.
7. **Be willing to be in action** and in living. Be purposeful and courageous in your decision-making because you really want to—and because you are willing to practice, to be precise, and to be wise!

Tools for Honoring You

Jo Lena Shares

Creating balance and order is essential in every area of your life. As previously mentioned, these "categories" include your health, finance, education/career, relationships/family, and spirituality/community. It's easy to get off track by stress, conflict, and events which can cause delay or discouragement. It's the nature of the human experience.

I recommend "making deposits" in each of these areas daily, as they will support you in growing your business because you are investing in your sanity, creating harmony, and taking care of your #1 business asset: YOU. You are the most important person in your life—and without you, you don't have a business to grow!

The Business of Massage

One of the ways I honor me through getting massages regularly. Sure, it's an art form—and for me, it's about business too. Without regular massages it's difficult for me to maintain a proper balance of peace of mind, flexibility of body, and the ability to cultivate, organize, maintain, and build my business relationships and business affairs.

When my muscles are tight in my neck, shoulders, and upper back, it's hard for me to move—and to think. I look stiff, I feel stiff, and I behave "stiffly." Being aware of your body and its needs is crucial to success. Too many times we ignore the warning signs and symptoms until they become "flashing lights" and emergencies.

Seven of the many benefits I receive from massage are:

1. Increased blood flow
2. Peace of mind
3. Clarity
4. Pain relief
5. Greater flexibility
6. Stress relief
7. Relaxation

I feel good when I get a massage because I'm also submitting— submitting to the fact that I need help, support, and care, which I can't necessarily provide for myself.

Getting a massage is a step in a good direction and at times, as a business owner, fitting my massages into my budget hasn't been easy. I found a solution that worked for me—I joined Massage Envy and now have the ability to budget my time, my money, and my relaxation in manageable ways.

I love their tag line *"…the feeling every body wants:"* how creative and true for me!

I mention them by name because some have turned giving massages into lucrative business ventures. When you think about your life, your passion, and your business, it's important to invest in something you believe in while you prosper. Because there are many academic and business books that talk about the pros and cons of franchises, I won't spend time discussing the technical aspects, I'll just say that I'm glad that the founders of Massage Envy created the business model that helps people: clients, and franchise owners, with their needs.

Some people go to spas and exchange business strategies, conduct informal business meetings, and such, similar to what some men do at the golf course. I personally don't do those things because I when I'm there, in the "world of massage," I finally let go and put other things on hold while I get down to handling my massage "business."

Through my travels around the U.S., Canada, the Caribbean, and the U.K., I have gotten some memorable massages. If you haven't guessed by now, I grew up in St. Louis, Missouri. When I'm in town, I enjoy my membership at the Webster Groves location of Massage Envy. I love it there—the people, the massages, and the atmosphere are all really good. The other thing I appreciate is the affordability. I like the idea of membership because I budget and schedule my massages just like other appointments.

Build confidence and assurance by eradicating any thoughts that are in between where you are and where you really want to be! Author Jewel Diamond Taylor wrote:

Beauty Tips for the Inner You
For attractive lips, speak words of kindness.
For beautiful eyes, seek out the good in other people
To feel lighter in your body, let go of stress and a need to control others.
To improve your ears, listen to the word of God.
Touch someone with your love.
Rather than focus on the thorns of life, smell the roses and count your blessings.
For poise, walk with knowledge and self-esteem.
To strengthen your arms, hug at least three people a day.

To strengthen your heart, forgive yourself and others.
Don't worry and hurry so much.
Rather walk this earth lightly and leave your mark.
"Stay in the Light"
Jewel Diamond Taylor

[Source: This poem by was sent to me through email a few years back. To get connected with more of Jewel Diamond Taylor's good works, please go to her website: http://www.donotgiveup.net]

"...Your body is the temple of the Holy Ghost which is in you..."
I Corinthians 6:19

Productivity Secrets

*"Not signing on to your email account can save you time
and help you stay focused."*

Donna Suggests

As I mentioned earlier, since there are so many daily tasks to do and we get caught up in our tasks list, and getting our emails answered that we forget that sitting in our office is not going to build relationships and alliances with those that are potential clients.

It's important to have office time and equally important to network and have alliances with those people you will do business with in the current year, or in the future.

I continuously meet women in business who are so passionate about their new product or services. What they have to offer will help other people. Yet, sometimes they are so caught up in working and forget that being around others helps to motivate them.

Ask yourself, "How much time do I spend on emails and tasks every week?" and "How much time do I spend networking and building relationships?" There can be a balance. I use time blocking in my business and thought I would share how it works for me in hopes that it might help you.

Using "Time Blocking" to Complete Tasks

I block out time in ½-day increments, along with some generic tasks. **Sam Black** is a Sales Trainer and Consultant who lives and operates through effective time blocking. She introduced me to time blocking during one of her telephone training courses. A few years later, **Cynthia Corel**, whose business is **"Right Hand for Hire,"** came to my office and helped me apply the practice to my situation and needs. I learned to be more productive because at the time, I was trying to do 2-hour time increments, and that wasn't working.

Here's an example of my current schedule:

1. Monday from 9 am—1 pm is office time, catching up on emails, and tasks. Monday from 1-5 pm is reserved for phone calls.

2. Tuesdays are my "Strategic Business Introduction" days. I schedule one in the morning and one in the late afternoon and then include a few one-on-one appointments in between.

3. Wednesday mornings are spent doing office work, afternoons and evenings are spent networking.

4. Thursday mornings are spent on either networking or office time and afternoons are for follow up phone calls and/or one-on-one appointments.

5. I typically keep Friday's for one-on-one appointments in the morning unless we have an Accelerated Networking event and afternoons for office work or play. Cynthia taught me to be more productive, focused, and organized. I've been working with her again now, in creating my game for women. Her calming spirit has allowed

us to make great progress in a short amount of time without being stressed out about it.

I have another suggestion that really helps me. Avoid emailing and picking up the phone (or cell phone) when you have other projects to complete. Choose projects that don't include the email and just don't open your inbox. It's easy to get caught up in messages and responding, and before you know if half the day is gone. Just tell yourself that the email or phone message can wait and will be there when you are done with your project. You might want to try an online stopwatch to help you track how much time you will spend on a project. www.online-stopwatch.com.

Mad Money to the Rescue

"..Every woman should have a stash..."

Wisdom from Banker Michelle Brown

Michelle Brown was born and raised in St. Louis, Missouri, where she currently resides. She is a mother of four and was a stay at home mom for many years. Michelle now manages a Fifth Third Bank Financial Center.

In addition to this, she has co-founded two companies that she co-manages. DEP LLC Event Planning and Small Business Development, and Believing in Excellence in Education, a character development course that teaches self-esteem and social skills.

Somehow she finds the time to manage it all while living and working in her passion—educating people on Finance.

Why did you choose the financial industry?

I've always been a money person, calculating interest and percentages. At the age of 10 or 11, while shopping with my mother—I was able to justify why my mom should buy the clothes because I was able to show her the value in the sales.

I figure that finance makes the world go around so why not be a part of something that will never go away. When I started my Master's Program, I made sure my emphasis was finance.

What are Three Things Entrepreneurs should avoid when it comes to banking?

1. **Fees.** If you do your research, you can find almost anything you need without a fee—you just have to shop around.

2. **Not establishing credit in the business name early on.** You must establish it—usually 2 years out, start establishing credit in the business name.

3. **Letting your personal credit go.** Too many small business owners have let their personal credit go. You will always have to be a signer and be able to guarantee your business loans—so if your personal credit is in disarray, you won't be able to get the loan. Keep tabs on your credit!

What is the biggest lesson you've learned as a woman in business?

"You get what you give." As I look back at my career, if you put effort in, you will see the fruits of your labor from that effort. Don't use being a woman as a crutch; if you really want something, you must go for it. It takes discipline; often times I stay up late and get up early. In addition to raising my children, being a full-time Financial Center Manager, co-running a non-profit and a small business, and my latest coo, teaching online classes (in finance) for a university. I may be a little sleepy, however, I'm making my financial goals, and I'm making a difference by sharing with my students. I love Nike's slogan "Just Do It™."

What is Mad Money?

When a woman is married (or not), every woman should have a stash of cash so that you have money to make a quick move if needed. No matter what—you always have to have options, and that's pretty hard if you don't have cash.

It also allows for you to formulate a savings plan—and a savings plan that not everyone knows about. When things happen or start going haywire you are able to use that account.

I recommend saving at least 8 months of monthly expenses—and that's how you can kind of gauge how much mad money you should have —so no matter what happens in your personal life, it won't negatively affect you or your business.

Start Good Habits Early

If you have children, children as young as 5 years old should start coming into the bank and begin making their own deposits, piggy banks in hand once a month.

What financial wisdom do you Really want entrepreneurs to know?

Pay down debt. If you pay it down, it'll free you up for you to save more. Make sure you have a fine balance—the old rule of thumb was, pay down your debt first before you start saving; however, because of the volatility in the economy in terms of jobs and such—and since people are losing jobs in record numbers—it's important to have money/savings available—even if that means paying minimum balances so that you can have some savings (cash) if needed.

How can you save when building a business?

It's about priorities—pay yourself first. Something has to come off the top for you. If you are bringing in $1 a day, a dime of that needs to go into a savings account.

You must eliminate fees of all kinds from your budget—overdraft and over the limit fees—you won't be able to save as much if you have fees and high interest rates.

About Relationships and Conduct Michelle Says:

1. Be careful of the company you keep—especially at work in terms of advancement because you will always be associated by the company you keep.
2. Dress for the position you want—appearance is pretty big.
3. If you are smarter than all of your friends, you need a new set of friends—you need others from whom you can learn.
4. What goes around comes around—in terms of how you handle different relationships so never burn bridges—it is the absolute truth. I have a really good friend who ironically was my manager and then I ended up being her manager. It's wonderful that we had a good relationship before.
5. Always do things ethically. If you know you aren't supposed to do it, don't.

I'm not sure how you manage it all! What is DEP, LLC?

Diva Event Planning DEP, LLC is a small business that I co founded and co manage. We do events, all types and sizes. In addition, we assist other small business owners elevate their businesses to the next level. Marketing, advertising, and yes, finances play a huge part in what we advise our business owners on at divaeventplanning.com—

You started a non-profit organization. What is it? And why did you start it?

I started "Believing in Excellence and Education" because I'm a mother and I saw a large disparity between what my children were being taught in my school district versus what other students were learning in districts that are more affluent.

In my opinion, we need those soft skills/life skills in order to compete in today's society—how to enunciate words properly, knowing which fork to use, keeping up with current events and more. Manners and proper etiquette wasn't being taught primarily because parents are more busy than ever. It's just not enough time in the day to go over every little thing. So, I decide to start a company that would focus on establishing these skills in the youth in our neighborhoods. By the time parents are finished working for the day, many parents don't have a lot of time to hone the soft skills children will need to compete in life so I created the bee program which teaches them those tools and skills.

Please visit Beelieve.org for more information about the program, or if you are interested in supporting the Bee program so that more children may attend.

Get connected with Michelle at
michelle@beelieve.org.

Have Fun

Jo Lena and Donna Chat

*"A happy heart is good medicine and a cheerful mind
works healing but a broken spirit dries up the bones."*
Proverbs 17:22

Jo Lena: I know a big part of who you are is centered on taking time
to play. Can you tell me why it is so important to you? And, why is
it so important to business women?

Donna: Fun is not just a concept it is an experience! Fun gives you
freedom because it lightens your disposition. It helps you release
stress and it gives you an outlet for creative expression. Time with
good friends can stimulate your creativity and others in your life will
appreciate it when you feel better too!

Jo Lena: One of the reasons I enjoy being with Donna is because
she's light in spirit and she knows how to have fun! Can you give us
some suggestions on how to have fun with friends?

Donna: Thank you, Jo Lena. We are busy women with what seems
to be not enough hours in the day yet we still need to manage our
fun just as we would our business. Here are some fun things to do
with your women friends.

Six Fun Things to do with Women Friends:

1. Form a dinner club where you can pick a theme, dress the part, and be willing to participate! How often you do it is up to you but I would recommend getting together every 4-6 weeks.

    a. Find out what your name means in Spanish and use it all night as you enjoy tapas, paella food from any of the Spanish speaking nations!

    b. Wear kimonos and eat sushi—ban the silverware and learn how to use chopsticks—especially if you don't know how—you'll entertain others especially if you are eating rice!

    c. Go to a French Restaurant and use your best "French Inspired" accent all night and "Voila!" Fun.

2. Pick a Game Night (Trivia, Cranium™, fabYOUstyle™ or Jacks anyone?)

3. Shopping sprees for you and your girlfriends! Creating "time limits, "color parameters" "themes" or expansive "rules" can make it really exciting. Get creative and silly—and if you don't personally need anything, gift your items to others!

4. Pick a new community each season and enjoy! Walk around and see holiday lights, enjoy pumpkin patches, apple orchards, free concerts in the park, art exhibits, and more.

5. Spa Days! Go to a spa or create a spa. Everyone gathers at one home, bringing the essentials for the day…your favorite polishes, lotions, candles, foot soaks, and warm towels. Fresh seasonal fruit with cucumber water, light snacks, and

great music. Take turns pampering yourself! This is a great way to get in some girlfriend time and get the pampering you deserve.

6. Progressive Dinners can be fun—Are you willing to try it?

    A Progressive is like "party hopping" with a twist. Everyone involved participates in creating, organizing, enjoying, and sharing the cost of chosen activities.

Pick about six friends and decide who will do what. It's all about appetizers, beverages, entrées, dessert, friends, and fun! Choose "pairs" of friends in the group to host a portion of the night. Get creative and enjoy the ride!

How the "progressive experience" could flow:

1. Pick a location with several restaurants in the area (within walking distance with good parking makes it even easier!). One pair can treat for appetizers and beverages at the first stop.

2. Stroll down to the next location where two or three treat for the entrees.

3. Finally, have some dessert—changing locations at this point gets your energy flowing and you can always split desserts and the check!

    On the other hand, you can do the same thing by going to one another's homes. One person does appetizers; one does salad, one entrée, and one dessert. If you want to have drinks, everybody brings something to contribute.

Having girlfriend time is so very important to me so I am in the process of creating a game for women to play called fabYOUstyle™. It is all about getting together, laughter and learning a little something about your personal style. Too many of us have lost the "little girl" inside and I hope this game helps women everywhere find the fun they are missing in their hectic, busy lives.

Give, Share, and Acknowledge

Donna and Jo Lena on Sharing

*"Giving is filling your spiritual pipeline. It starts
with God giving us grace, mercy, and the capacity
to receive. If you really want to be successful, it
takes the willingness to give to Him as well."*
Jo Lena Johnson

The more you can give and help others, or promote others, their events, or causes, the more it will come back to you in untold ways. Whatever your beliefs, the principle of tithing is important. Tithing can include money, time, or talent, and it works. Starting by giving to God, the Source and Supplier, is the biggest investment you can make. Starting each day with praise, thanksgiving, and acknowledgement keeps you connected and fills your storehouse at the same time.

When growing your business, taking time to care for the "entire you" is certain to keep you grounded, relaxed, and willing to give.

We suggest investing an hour a week in helping a woman to grow her business. This could be strategic planning, brainstorming, filing, faxing, or joining her at a monthly meeting. Doing things together usually assists both parties.

> *"And God is able to make all grace abound toward*
> *you; that ye, always having all sufficiency in all*
> *good things, may abound to every good work:"*
> *2* Corinthians 9:8

The eWomenNetwork Foundation is one of Donna's favorite ways to "give." Every year many chapters provide scholarships to at least one young woman between the ages of 20 and 29. This scholarship pays for them to attend the annual conference where they receive training and make some incredible connections. Donna says the conference can be a life-changing experience for those afforded the opportunity, as the recipient gets to see how successful women interact, build relationships, and create alliances.

Donna shares about eWomenNetwork

Sandra Yancey, founder of eWomenNetwork has taught me to give first and to share always. To really understand that the *reason for the network is to share our resources and connections so that others are successful.*

This organization has made such a profound difference in my life and in the lives of so many others. It gives us a way to meet and connect; learn and grow; and develop and build our lives. I'm also able to give to the community through activities of the foundation.

Attending conferences is an extension of our local activities and the experience is phenomenal. Being able to meet successful professional women from all over the country has broadened my connections and positioned me for future endeavors. And, getting out of town and having fun are invaluable!

Each time I return from the annual eWomenNetwork Conference, I am really enthusiastic, inspired, and ready to get into action. During the summer of 2009, not only did I make some great connections but also heard some incredible speakers. One who has inspired me is **Peggy McColl**. She shared about a time when she was divorced, living on very little, and not sure how she would sell the 3000 books she had just had delivered to her dining room. I was so impressed that she was able to sell all of her 3000 books within 3 days simply by asking people in her life to help get the word out. This is the kind of network I have built at eWomenNetwork and for that, I am very thankful.

A great way to give is to share, teach, and show what you know!

Think of other women in your circle that need your help and then take time to help them…help them to become more successful. Asking, "How can I help you?" is a great start.

As we've stated before, relationships matter! And because everyone can benefit from experienced wisdom, trusted sources and good people, we really want you to know that we haven't been able to overcome obstacles and build our businesses in a vacuum—many people have supported us along the way.

> *"Tithing is a principle and if everyone adds*
> *their little piece, it is like magic dust."*
> Donna Gamache

Please Remember

Take the time, create the space, forget the perfection, and choose to let go for 65 minutes—some of the best relationships, ideas, and books happen that way!

On the following pages, we share a few resources with you, including organizations, websites, and some of our friends.

To Your Success, Donna and Jo Lena

Feed Your Mind with Good Books

"A gift is a precious stone in the eyes of him that hath it: whither so ever it turneth, it prospereth."
Proverbs 17:8

1. *The Power is Within You* by Louise Hay

2. *Heal Your Body* by Louise Hay

3. *Zero Limits* by Joe Vitale

4. *The Be (Happy) Attitudes* by Robert Schuller

5. *Be The Media* by David Mathison

6. *The Irresistible Offer* by Mark Joyner

7. *The Power of Focus* by Jack Canfield

8. *A Whole New Mind* by Daniel Pink

9. *The E-Myth Revisited* by Michael Gerber

10. *Womenomics* by Claire Shipman and Katty Kay

11. *If You Really Want to Live, Be Extraordinary!* by Jo Lena Johnson and Dr. Lee Roy Jefferson

12. *How to Be Like Women of Influence* by Pat and Ruth Williams with Michael Mink

13. *How to be Like Women of Power* by Pat and Ruth Williams with Michael Mink

14. *The Holy Bible ~ God's Instruction Book for Life*

Your Communication: It's Your Choice!

Jo Lena Recommends

Presenting yourself in a way which is becoming, professional, and which sends the message you intend takes practice. One of the hardest things to combat at home, school, and work is expressing yourself when you are upset, confused, or just don't know what to say. It can be even tougher when you have something to say, and just can't seem to "get it out."

I occasionally submit articles to magazines and one of my favorites is *Breathe Again* magazine, founded by my friend Nicole Cleveland. This is an excerpt from one of the magazine's readers, and my response, may it be of support to you, as well.

> *Dear Jo Lena,*
>
> *I have the hardest time with oral communication in front of groups of people. When I'm in front of a group of people, I can't get the words to come out right... I know what I want say, but it just doesn't come out right. What am I doing wrong? I'm not a shy person. Help please! Christine*
>
> *Dear Christine:*
>
> *Thanks so much for your question. Rest assured there is nothing wrong with you, and it's understandable that you may not be shy. The majority of people on the planet rank public speaking as one of the hardest challenges they believe they can't overcome.*

It seems that you haven't gained confidence in speaking in front of groups of people. If you are concentrating on "not getting the words right," guess what? The "words won't be right!" So, if you are willing, I have a few suggestions:

1. *Concentrate on a recurring meeting or situation in which you know the players, the typical occurrences, and what type of info you have wanted to share the last two or three times you have been there—and held back. Once you have come up with two-three thoughts or expressions, practice saying them in front of a friend or partner and start by saying, "There are twp points I'd like to make" and then make them—showing confidence, even if you don't feel confident.*

2. *After you have shown and experienced confidence, PLAN on providing your input at the next meeting. Even if it's not the exact info that you practiced, don't say "I have a couple of things to share" do say "I have one thing to add" or "I have two things I'd like to mention." Be clear, focused, concise, and remember to smile!*

3. *After you have overcome your discomfort with speaking in front of the group, and have gained success in this area, PLAN to contribute at your next two to four upcoming meetings, adding input from notes that you have written in advance or during the meeting: small but impactful tidbits which will add value, information, or perhaps another perspective which the group would not have should you continue to clam up.*

4. *Remember, wherever you are, you matter. A silent you, focused on what you don't do well remains invisible and non-contributory. A confident, willing, and practiced you makes for a trusted associate who is looked to for expertise. It's all a process and practice does not make perfect—practice makes skilled!*

It's your choice! Thanks for the question, keep them coming, and I know you will have Absolute Good Success!

Jo Lena Johnson

Web Tools for Entrepreneurs

For your use, and to your success and discovery!

You could spend a week searching for materials and tools to support your business. There are offerings, articles, and more eNewsletters available than your inbox can support! This list is a "gift" from us to you. We have found these websites to be helpful, timesaving, and great technological resources for most concerns of business owners. Each site offers slightly difference perspectives, styles, and even some non-traditional opportunities to participate and connect globally.

ALLBUSINESS.COM
   http://www.allbusiness.com/
AllBusiness.com offers practical articles, great resources, and a connection to Dun and Bradstreet. It includes business directory listings, guides, and even a business association. It's a "connection" to the businesses that do business and a must visit if you don't have a Dun and Bradstreet number!

BUSINESS OWNER'S TOOLKIT
   http://www.toolkit.cch.com/
An excellent guide to starting, financing, marketing, growing, and dispensing of your business. Their name says it all—and their resources are outstanding. The site is easy to navigate and they have a sister site called Financial Planning Toolkit.

ENTREPRENEUR.COM

http://www.entrepreneur.com/

Entrepreneur.com is part of Entrepreneur Magazine's extensive network. It offers insights for start-ups and small business entrepreneurs; it's just great.

ENTREPRENEURSHIP.ORG

http://www.entrepreneurship.org/

The Ewing Marion Kauffman Foundation and the U.S. Commerce Department's International Trade Administration (ITA) have formed a new public-private partnership focused on leveraging best practices in entrepreneurial leadership to advance economic growth around the world. The goal of this partnership is to assist all nations in developing the environment to allow entrepreneurs to organize and operate a business venture, create wealth, and employ people.

MOREBUSINESS.COM

http://www.morebusiness.com/

MoreBusiness.com is an award-winning, one-stop resource website for entrepreneurs. Created in 1994, MoreBusiness.com is filled with sample business plans, marketing plans, templates, sample contracts, and business agreements to help entrepreneurs start and grow a small business.

SMARTBIZ.COM

http://www.smartbiz.com/

Smartbiz.com offers many resources to help you run your business; it's especially helpful for offering practical management solutions.

YOUNG AMERICAS BUSINESS TRUST

> http://www.ybiz.com/

Young Americas Business Trust promotes social and economic development in the Western Hemisphere and elsewhere through programs, projects, and activities focused on helping to create and advance efforts to improve the quality of life of youth and young adults, especially those living in or near poverty. Connect with others who are doing what it takes to make a difference.

ENTREPRENEURS' ORGANIZATION

> http://www.eonetwork.org

As a global, non-profit educational organization for young entrepreneurs, Young Entrepreneurs' Organization (YEO) strives to help its members build upon their successes through an array of educational and networking opportunities.

The site is dynamic and so is the EO's business structure: with over 7,300 business owners in 42 countries, the organization was founded by a group of young entrepreneurs to learn and grow from each other, "leading to greater business success and an enriched personal life." We are sharing more information about this site to inspire you to take action in your own vision, mission, and core values as well. The organization is an example of what can happen when talented, qualified, inspired, and willing people get connected.

EO's Vision: To build the world's most influential community of entrepreneurs.

EO's Mission: Engage leading entrepreneurs to learn and grow.

EO's Core Values:

- **Boldly Go!**—Bet on your own abilities

- **Thirst for Learning**—Be a student of opportunity

- **Make a Mark**—Leave a legacy

- **Trust and Respect**—Build a safe haven for learning and growth

- **Cool**—Create, seek out and celebrate once-in-a-lifetime experiences

You can use the example above to start to define or redefine your own vision, mission, and core values. This is a nice, simple model and we appreciate their placing it on their website.

Most truly successful business owners know that continuous learning is required to excel. We suggest that you actively engage in learning opportunities like reading, workshops, coaching, and training sessions.

Small Business Considerations
Directly from Wikipedia.org

Readers, when it was time to sum up a few things for you, and to give some definitions, more considerations, and a few statistics, we used the internet. Though very slightly edited, this entire section comes from the Internet page http://en.wikipedia.org/wiki/Small_business.

It serves as a testimony for the wealth of information found on the internet, for the depth of the overall scope of what it really means to be successful as a small business owner, and it speaks to the value of the wisdom shared by the women in this book, who addressed many of these concerns simply through sharing their experience.

You have a choice.

If you really want to be successful, get connected with you, first. Once you know what you really want; get connected with those who will be forthcoming and helpful to you and to themselves; and get and stay connected with tools, resources, and with proven track records of success. Innovate, take risks, plan, be true to yourself, and choose your path. You have the MAP…and the information shared below provides some "monumental considerations" along the way.

From Wikipedia.org:

A **small business** is a business that is privately owned and operated, with a small number of employees and relatively low volume of sales. Small businesses are normally privately owned corporations, partnerships, or sole proprietorships. The legal definition of "small" varies by country and by industry. In the United States the Small Business Administration establishes small business size standards on an industry-by-industry basis, but generally specifies a small business as having fewer than 500 employees for manufacturing businesses and less than $7 million in annual receipts for most nonmanufacturing businesses.

In addition to number of employees, other methods used to classify small companies include annual sales (turnover), value of assets and net profit (balance sheet), alone or in a mixed definition.

Small businesses are usually not dominant in their field of operation.

Small businesses are common in many countries, depending on the economic system in operation. Typical examples include: convenience stores, other small shops (such as a bakery or delicatessen), hairdressers, tradesmen, lawyers, accountants, restaurants, guest houses, photographers, small-scale manufacturing etc.

The smallest businesses, often located in private homes, are called microbusinesses (term used by international organizations such as the World Bank and the International Finance Corporation).

There is a notable trend to further segment different-sized microbusinesses; for instance, the term Very Small Business is now being used to refer to businesses that are the smallest of the smallest, such as those operated completely by one person or by 1-3 employees.

Advantages of Small Business

- A small business can be started at a very low cost and on a part-time basis.

- Small business is also well suited to internet marketing because it can easily serve specialized niches.

- Adapting to change is crucial in business and particularly small business; not being tied to any bureaucratic inertia, it is typically easier to respond to the marketplace quickly.

- Small business proprietors tend to be intimate with their customers and clients, which results in greater accountability and maturity.

- Independence is another advantage of owning a small business.

- One survey of small business owners showed that 38% of those who left their jobs at other companies said their main reason for leaving was that they wanted to be their own bosses.

- Freedom to operate independently is a reward for small business owners. In addition, many people desire to make their own decisions, take their own risks, and reap the rewards of their efforts.

- Small business owners have the satisfaction of making their own decisions within the constraints imposed by economic and other environmental factors.

- However, entrepreneurs have to work very long hours and understand that ultimately their customers are their bosses.

Several organizations also provide help for the small business sector, such as the Internal Revenue Service's Small Business and Self-Employed One-Stop Resource.

Problems Faced by Small Businesses

- Small businesses often face a variety of problems related to their size.

- A frequent cause of bankruptcy is undercapitalization. This is often a result of poor planning rather than economic conditions - it is common rule of thumb that the entrepreneur should have access to a sum of money at least equal to the projected revenue for the first year of business in addition to his anticipated expenses.

For example, if the prospective owner thinks that he will generate $100,000 in revenues in the first year with $150,000 in start-up expenses, then he should have no less than $250,000 available. Failure to provide this level of funding for the company could leave the owner liable for all of the company's debt should he end up in bankruptcy court, under the theory of undercapitalization.

- In addition to ensuring that the business has enough capital, the small business owner must also be mindful of contribution margin (sales minus variable costs).

To break even, the business must be able to reach a level of sales where the contribution margin equals fixed costs.

- When they first start out, many small business owners under price their products to a point where even at their maximum capacity, it would be impossible to break even. Cost controls or price increases often resolve this problem.

- In the United States, some of the largest concerns of small business owners are insurance costs (such as liability and health), rising energy costs and taxes.

- **The 'Entrepreneurial Myth' or E-Myth.** The mythic assumption is that an expert in a given technical field will also be expert at running that kind of business. Additional business management skills are needed to keep a business running smoothly.

Marketing the Small Business

Small businesses typically find themselves strapped for time but in order to create a continual stream of new business, they must work on marketing their business every day.

Common marketing techniques for small business include networking, word of mouth, customer referrals, yellow pages directories, television, radio, outdoor (roadside billboards), print, email marketing, and internet. Electronic media like TV can be quite expensive and is normally intended to create awareness of a product or service.

Many small business owners find internet marketing more affordable. Google Ad Words and Yahoo! Search Marketing are two popular options of getting small business products or services in front of motivated Web searchers. Advertising on niche sites can also be effective, but with the long tail of the internet, it can be time intensive to advertise on enough sites to garner an effective reach.

Creating a business Web site has become increasingly affordable with many do-it-yourself programs now available for beginners. A Web site can provide significant marketing exposure for small businesses when marketed through the Internet and other channels.

Social media has proven to be very useful in gaining additional exposure for many small businesses.

Franchise Businesses

Franchising is a way for small business owners to benefit from the economies of scale of the big corporation (franchiser). McDonald's restaurants, TrueValue hardware stores, and NAPA Auto Parts stores are examples of a franchise. The small business owner can leverage a strong brand name and purchasing power of the larger company while keeping their own investment affordable. However, some franchisees conclude that they suffer the "worst of both worlds" feeling they are too restricted by corporate mandates and lack true independence.

Small Business Bankruptcy

When small business fails, the owner may file bankruptcy. In most cases, this can be handled through a personal bankruptcy filing. Corporations can file bankruptcy, but if it is out of business and valuable corporate assets are likely to be repossessed by secured creditors there is little advantage to going to the expense of a corporate bankruptcy. Many states offer exemptions for small business assets so they can continue to operate during and after personal bankruptcy. However, corporate assets are normally not exempt; hence, it may be more difficult to continue operating an incorporated business if the owner files bankruptcy.

Certification and Trust

Building trust with new customers can be a difficult task for a new and establishing business. Some organizations like the Better Business Bureau and the International Charter now offer Small Business Certification, which certifies the quality of the services and goods produced and can encourage new and larger customers. These services may require a few hours of work, but a certification may reassure potential customers.

Sources of funding

Small businesses use several sources available for start-up capital:

- Self-financing by the owner through cash, equity loan on his or her home, and or other assets.

- Loans from friends or relatives

- Grants from private foundations

- Personal Savings

- Private stock issue

- Forming partnerships

- Angel Investors

- Banks

- SME finance, including Collateral based lending and Venture capital, given sufficiently sound business venture plans

Some small businesses are further financed through credit card debt - usually a poor choice, given that the interest rate on credit cards is often several times the rate that would be paid on a line of credit or bank loan. Many owners seek a bank loan in the name of their business, however banks will usually insist on a personal guarantee by the business owner. In the United States, the Small Business Administration (SBA) runs several loan programs that may help a small business secure loans. In these programs, the SBA guarantees a portion of the loan to the issuing bank and thus relieves the bank of some of the risk of extending the loan to a small business. The SBA also requires business owners to pledge personal assets and sign as a personal guarantee for the loan.

Canadian small businesses can take advantage of federally funded programs and services. See Federal financing for small businesses in Canada (grants and loans).

Business Networks and Advocacy Groups

Small businesses often join or come together to form organizations to advocate for their causes or to achieve economies of scale that larger businesses benefit from, such as the opportunity to buy cheaper health insurance in bulk. These organizations include local or regional groups such as Chambers of Commerce, as well as national or international industry-specific organizations. Such groups often serve a dual purpose, as business networks to provide marketing and connect members to potential sales leads and suppliers, and also as advocacy groups, bringing together many small businesses to provide a stronger voice in regional or national politics.

The largest regional small business group in the United States is the Council of Smaller Enterprises, located in Greater Cleveland.[9]

[Source: http://en.wikipedia.org/wiki/Small_business]

Online Business Resources

1. http://www.guru.com

2. http://www.elance.com

3. http://www.vervante.com

   A product fulfillment company that packages and sends your books, products, etc. to your clients—and they provide great customer service!

4. http://www.lulu.com

   Offers book self-publishing, and print on demand services

5. http://www.mashable.com

   Online magazine of social media for entrepreneurs)

6. http://www.inc.com

7. http://www.fastcompany.com

8. http://www.business20.com

Section Five

THE REARVIEW MIRROR
MIRROR
Reflections

How the Authors Are Giving ~
Thanks to You!

IF YOU REALLY WANT TO BE SUCCESSFUL IN BUILDING YOUR BUSINESS—CHOOSE TO GIVE FREELY! Young people can use some support! This book is dedicated to showing them how much they matter. Each of these organizations are worthy causes—helping women and youth to build esteem, experiences, and a better quality of life.

Ten percent (each) of our personal profits from these book sales will go to these organizations because we know the importance of giving. We encourage you to give and to share: who you are, your talent, your time, and your resources with these groups or others like them in your area.

Donna supports the eWomenNetwork Foundation. Through the generous donations of eWomenNetwork members and guests, we are able to give back to non-profits that support women and children. To learn more, please visit www.ewomennetworkfoundation.org.

Jo Lena supports the Urban Opportunities Program in conjunction with the St. Louis City 4-H Youth Development Program. 4-H is a community of young people across America learning leadership, citizenship, and life skills. The St. Louis City 4-H program engages youth in meaningful experiences that promote education, leadership, and community service. As a result, youth will become positive, productive, and responsible citizens in the future. If you *really* want to grow, giving time, school supplies, cash donations, and resources will grow your heart and their experiences! Get Connected by emailing Dr. Jody J. Squires at squiresj@missouri.edu.

How this Book Came to Be

Reflections from Jo Lena

In August of 2009, Donna and I sat down for what turned out to be a life-altering afternoon. We had been trying to connect in person for weeks and weeks, and we almost postponed our meeting again. I was late and stressed—and she was understanding, patient, and fabulously put together, as always. We just really wanted to enjoy some "friend time." Not only did we create friend time, we also, spontaneously created the outline for this book.

Donna and I were at crossroads in our lives. Both of us have been successful in business ventures, handling schedules, managing tasks, and in conducting consultations and training sessions of various sorts. Unbeknownst to us, we were in similar places regarding our personal lives, professional desires, and the need for additional resources. We both agreed that if we had more, we could give more.

This book was born out of a desire for greater support, new friendship, and a vision of success, blessings, and resources to live and give to others.

Donna, like most of us, wears many hats, and what I really admire is that she makes being a successful business woman look simple and fashionable! When I asked her how she does it, she was kind enough to share what she does to "keep it all together."

And that summer day in August 2009, at St. Louis Bread Company, an alliance was formed!

We hope that you have discovered steps you can take to build confidence, create professional relationships, and enjoy life while growing your business.

Dying a Slow Death

"…I went out and bought a Macintosh computer
with over 30 Megs of ram for over $5,000…I
didn't have a printer or anything else."

Life Experience from Donna Gamache

I'm Donna Gamache and I've been a business owner since I was 26 years old. I needed money and I needed an option that allowed me to stay home with my two sons. I did Tupperware and I found out that I didn't like the home parties and the sales. So, I started making homemade crafts. First was cross stitch, then basket weaving, then my own line of soft sculptured dolls. I traveled the craft circuit for about 5 years selling my homemade wares. The biggest compliment I received while selling my dolls was from an employee of Xavier Roberts (founder of the Cabbage Patch Dolls) who threatened to sue me for making dolls that looked like theirs. I knew there was no way my dolls could look exactly like theirs because I couldn't make two dolls that looked exactly the same. So I smiled and said, "Bring it on." And I never heard from them again!

I'm really committed to helping women create fun and/or recapture the fun, in life. In addition to being a part of the "If You Really Want to" book series with Jo Lena Johnson, I have created the fabYOUstyle™ game for women, which helps us have fun and bond with girlfriends while learning about our personal styles. This game will help you find the inner fun girl that you may have lost in the hectic and fast paced life of entrepreneurship.

Through the years I've done many things; I became a school administrator in order to work during the same hours that my sons were in school and during that time, I found that I had a real aptitude for the computer and began training my co-workers.

I then worked in a design firm creating ads and began to use graphic design programs. At that point, I was working at an advertising firm in Greenville, South Carolina; it was the late 80's and we found out that my mother-in-law had Alzheimer's disease. My husband at that time and I made a decision to move our family to St. Louis to care for her, and someone at my firm recommended that I apply at for a position at Maritz, a big firm in St. Louis. I did apply at Maritz and was offered two different positions, but at a starting position and salary that wasn't what I really wanted or deserved to make.

So, I went out and bought a Macintosh computer with over 30 Megs of ram for over $5,000 (I didn't have a printer or anything else) and started my first IT company called Desk Top Consulting. After only 6 months of owning my own business, I was contracted by Maritz Performance Improvement to train their entire staff of graphic artists and word processing professionals. This time, I was making what I wanted when working with them. For about 5 years I was doing the type of work I enjoyed and making the amount of money that supported my life style.

Then, in 1995 my whole world changed—I got a divorce. There I was with my two teenage sons and I had a knee-jerk reaction. In order to "afford" health benefits and such, I folded my company and went back into corporate America as a consultant. After three years of IT training and development, I realized I didn't like working in corporate America. I married Steve Gamache in 2001, and my life and world changed—again.

One day, during the first year of our marriage, I came home and said to Steve, "My spirit is dying inside of me." He said "Okay, you don't have to go back." He gifted me the opportunity to start my own (now third) business, the Right Results, the company I have today. He said he would take care of the finances at home while I started the business. I was relieved and grateful because I knew I had his support to get the company off the ground. Had I not been married to Steve at that time I would have been forced to stay in the corporate consulting arena—dying a slow death every single day because I didn't feel like my work was making a difference for and with people.

I know it sounds like my husband rescued me—and in a way, he did. Daily I prayed for the strength, courage, and wisdom to figure out how I was going to be successful in living my life's purpose. I believe my prayers were answered because I had a connection with my spirit—which said, "Killing me softly is not okay." The material support that my marriage offered certainly made me more "comfortable" in leaving the corporate world again, yet I believe that faith and the yearning in my soul to meet and connect with people drew me toward my higher goals.

My life was not and has not been "easy" yet, with focus, learning new skills, building new relationships, and collaborating with others, I consider myself blessed and am honored to be able to serve people— and especially women, through my current entrepreneurial pursuit.

The Right Results is a style consulting company—personal style as well as business style. I help women to make the best first impression they possibly can—both in the way they dress and in the way they present and brand themselves. I don't actually create the business cards and brochures; however, I work with them to analyze and to review their marketing materials to make sure they are in keeping with the image and the message they really want to convey.

What I *Really* Want for Women…

*It's about others when I am there. It's
about having a "we attitude."*
Donna Gamache

I *really* want women to live in harmony.

Notice I didn't say balance because I truly think it is difficult to live a balanced life. What I mean is that there are always going to be times when you have more of one thing on your plate. For example, when you are working on deadlines for your business, the scales are going to tip on the business side and less on the family and friend side. When we live in harmony, things may not be balanced but we can live knowing that our mind, body, and spirit are in sync. This means taking time each day to meditate, eat right, and get plenty of sleep.

I also want women to:

1. Have more confidence, be more self-assured
2. Develop or strengthen their inner strength and beauty
3. Experience freedom from fear of who they think you are and experience acceptance of yourself as a dynamic woman

Wise Women Who Have Influenced My Life

Virginia Waters (my mom) has influenced me in so many ways, with her energetic, fun spirit, and her tenacity. At age 50, she went back to school and got her degree. At age 73, she took dance lessons and was in competitions, winning them with her younger partner. I just appreciate how much she continues to give and share her loving care with our family.

Sandra Yancey has taught me so much about giving and sharing. Watching her create a network for women in business has taught me much about how to stay in the game, and to have the determination it takes to succeed and do it with grace and ease.

Joyce Meyer has influenced me in my faith with her straightforwardness about Biblical principles. I like a woman who tells it how it is.

Karen Hoffman has been a strong influence, teaching me how to be a connector and to be collaborative. I so appreciate the unconditional support I get from her.

Peggy McColl has influenced me to not let fear get in my way…to do what it is that I want to do and to know that if it's the right thing for me, nothing can stand in my way. She is also providing the tools for me to take my game and this book to market in a viral way.

Michelle Johnson has taught me the importance of self-care. She remains a calming, harmonious presence in my life and I'm so very grateful for her.

Lethia Owens is a powerhouse of energy and resourcefulness. Her knowledge and wisdom in the area of personal branding has taught me the value of online resource, and I'm so glad to know her.

My girlfriends Kerry, Linda, Cari, Patty, Karen, and Kathy who have laughed with me through all the Mardi Gras parades, progressive dinners, and Sweet Potato Queen trips.

I'm excited to Get Connected with you! For fun with my new fabYOUstyle™ game or to speak with you or your group connect with me at dgamache@rightresults.net.

My Mouth, My Mission, and Me

"People have loved me in spite of my mistakes and shortcomings—and I'm so very grateful!"

Life Experience from Jo Lena Johnson

I have learned the devastating effects of conflict (lack of or miscommunication) firsthand in professional and personal relationships, as part of the fabric of society, and of some business structures. Thus, I have not been an ideal corporate America poster child. Yet, when people are willing to change the way we communicate and the way we lead, everyone benefits—and I am committed to creating understanding.

I'm often asked how I became a business owner. My answer is that I don't ever remember "deciding," it just happened.

My mom, Sandy, married Bill McHugh when I was 4 years old, and together they raised my brother, William, Jr. and me. Thanks to them, I was allowed and encouraged to work in order to earn additional money to get some of the things I really wanted. By giving me a $2 a week allowance, I learned the value of money, and that $2 didn't go very far on its own. I emphasize "really wanted" because, in my experience, whatever one "really wants" usually takes commitment, effort, practice, and often giving up of things that we don't want. At a young age, it meant that I was willing to figure out what to do, and how to do, in order to achieve, or get to the end result.

I learned how to turn my skills into business ventures. Sometimes I earned extra money and sometimes I didn't—I was just excited to be helping, learning, and working. There were always projects going on around our house and garage. I participated in everything I could, from filling out every one of the Publisher's Clearing House Sweepstakes entries, to dicing vegetables, to going "junking" with mom at antique places and dad at junkyards for car parts. My mom is an artist, and I would serve as her "glitter and glue assistant" when she would create posters, banners, and signs for various clients, and when dad wasn't at his law office, I would be in the garage as his "wrench and tool specialist" when something, anything, needed repair.

On my twelfth birthday, my father, Kenneth Johnson (a wise and successful entrepreneur in the insurance industry), sent me $100 and I was so excited! I don't know if Mom had told him but, I had my eye on a black and white RCA television, which cost $99.99, and there was no way I could have earned enough to pay that amount on my own. I was ready to go to the store immediately. I remember being discouraged before getting to the checkout counter when I learned that I needed an extra $5 for the taxes; my mom loaned it to me! That TV was one of the best "investments" I ever made; and 27 years later, that TV is in her basement and it still works!

Three things happened during my senior year of high school (Riverview Gardens Class of 1988!) that would end up being indicators of my life's path. My peers voted me the "Most Spirited" and the "Bossiest" (female) awards. And at graduation, the faculty and staff gave me the "Service" Award, right after the Valedictorian and the Salutatorian.

While I attended the University of Missouri-Columbia, I had a four-year summer internship at the St. Louis Airport Marriott

Hotel through my participation in the INROADS Leadership Program. INROADS taught me discipline, accountability, and the fundamentals of behaving like a responsible leader, as we spent Saturdays dressed in business attire learning skills and tools for life in corporate America. During the week, I was part of the hotel's marketing team and worked in every department. While working side by side with people in the bakery, housekeeping, sales, and reservations, I noticed the sense of superiority that some had, and the spirit of humility and service which others possessed. I made up my mind that the hotel would not function if it wasn't cleaned and in proper working order—and that the "executives" needed to understand that they wouldn't have a room to sell if they did not appreciate the people who were "really" running the facility.

During college, I also worked at Dad's law office on holiday breaks, in between substitute teaching at my alma mater, Riverview Gardens. I love the intent of the law—and the just application of it; I even considered becoming a lawyer but felt that I wasn't disciplined enough to make it through law school. It was during that time I started conducting impromptu workshops with students, where I taught them things about college campus life, school supplies like buckets and shower shoes, and how to apply for student financial aid. I just wanted them to know that they had choices in life, and by using the blackboard, chalk, and a little imagination, we had meaningful interactive sessions that taught them and me the importance of encouraging people to create dreams, and becoming prepared to live them.

After graduation, instead of working for the Marriott, who had gone through major managerial changes in my four summers, I worked for Trans World Airlines (TWA) in the reservations department. This is significant for several reasons: I didn't want to work at the hotel and get involved in the politics and what I felt were attitudes of elitism; I didn't want to be "boxed in" to corporate life because I saw that people just weren't satisfied; also, I didn't have any money and I was unsure of how to proceed.

With my college degree and other accomplishments, it would have been easy to ignore the phone call I received telling me about the opportunities at TWA, yet there was something appealing about the flying for almost "free." After investigating, I enrolled in "reservations school," got hired, and completed my 90 days' probation; I had great, great benefits; and I helped solve all types of problems daily while honing my customer service skills; I had lots of flexibility; and earned less than $6 per hour! So, I continued my "entrepreneurial pursuits" and could fly anywhere in the United States for $20 round trip!

Using creative scheduling, affordable flight privileges, and great relationships with former college friends, in a year's time I moved to Los Angeles—I was liberated! I had several jobs and projects in marketing; made many lifelong friends; I married and divorced my college sweetheart; studied to become a teacher through my church, led by (Minister) Della Reese; and I started Absolute Good Marketing, Promotion and Events as a creative way to earn additional income. And eventually, while I enjoyed marketing products, I found myself wanting to make more of a positive impact in people's lives.

To sum up this non-traditional path that is my life, I want you to know that I was really proud of the "Spirited and Bossiest" awards because I knew them to be true about myself. I just didn't know at the time how difficult "bossy" would be when dealing in life relationships, as a manager of people, and in corporate America later in life. What I most want is for people to know how much they matter. Most of what I teach is just practical, principle-based "how to's" and "how not to's."

Eventually I started the Training and Life Skills Division of Absolute Good. I supplemented my AG income by working with some of the world's best training companies like FranklinCovey and Vital Smarts. I didn't have a business plan, investors, financing or formal advisors, or a even vision statement—I was simply driven by intention, resourcefulness, and the confidence that somehow things would work out because I was organized, a hard worker, and had many experiences in life which I thought, if shared, would help me and everybody else, to succeed.

The good news is that all along the way parents, teachers, friends, informal mentors, and (some) bosses have appreciated my sincerity and worked with me to improve in areas needing improvement. This "big mouth" that has gotten me into trouble has also served to communicate to people what not to do! Finally, I started the *"If You Really Want to"* series because so many people say they want things and have no idea how to start or how to finish.

I want people to have the help they really need.

I really want people to learn how to communicate and how to lead in ways which are beneficial to self-esteem, creating understanding, and are based on principles and values.

I want people to know that we each need each other and that with guidance, preparation, training, and sharing experiences, each person becomes wise. Once we learn to be consistent in application of that wisdom, <u>we succeed</u>.

Though I have touched over 65,000 people in person, I'm hoping that the wisdom found in these books help millions more.

Wise Women Who Have Influenced My Life

Sandra McHugh—My mother took a part-time job when I was eight years old because I was chubby—she knew my self-esteem would be better if she could purchase "chubby girl" clothes which would fit me better. Those clothes were more costly than regular clothes and she wanted the very best for me. Tenacious, proud, brilliant, and caring, my mom is a talented self-taught fine artist and I'm honored to represent her body of work. Get Connected and see mom's work at www.sandymchugh.com.

Jerry Eileen Perry—Aunt Jerry is one of the kindest, most humble and admirable people I know. *Aunt Jerry passed during the editing of this book, on March 30, 2010. I was developing a children's book series called "Aunt Jerry Loves Blue and So Can You" at the time. I'm honored for the time we spent together and I wish all people, young and matured could have an opportunity to have an "Aunt Jerry." Rest in peace.*

Ruth Williams—Helped me to be a more effective trainer when we were facilitators for the FranklinCovey organization. She shows me that it's possible to be talented, ambitious, a woman of faith, and 100% committed to family—while maintaining a sunny disposition and a healthy, joyful marriage. With her loving husband Pat, they have raised 19 children, and are thrilled with the grandchildren too. Ruth still finds the time to teach, help others, and complete her PhD! Besides wearing St. John suits, she is also a published author several times over. From the time I met her, she held a special place in my heart and when I get discouraged, I smile and keep going when I think of her.

Maida Coleman—Maida taught me that politics isn't really about winning—it's about willingness to take action where you see a need. She's brilliant, humble, and a woman of integrity. A former state senator for Missouri, a women's advocate, a writer, lecturer, and a civil servant, Maida offers a heart of gold, courage, and experienced leadership.

La Tia King is a lifelong friend shows me daily how to lead with my heart. She's amazing. Philanthropy, service, and kindness are in her DNA. I appreciate her approach to life and to building real relationships.

Paula M. Long is a lifelong friend/sister who is loving, kind, and who works hard no matter what. I have been particularly inspired by her pursuit to master the art of sign language. She uses her considerable talents, her interests, and her hands to uplift the hearing impaired and it is truly a wonderful sight to behold.

(Ms.) Daryle Brown is one of the brightest, most practical and talented people I have ever met. She has been an anchorperson, writer, and producer in Hollywood for years. I admire the quality of her work, her abilities, and her heart to report (the news) that people really need to know. There are no words to describe our friendship/sisterhood. All I can say is God answers prayer by placing people in our lives for seasons and reasons. She supports my personal and business "adventures" unconditionally.

W. Samantha Newman of Sunti Designs is a very good illustrator. I am so glad to have her in my life because she understands what her clients need, and delivers. Every business person needs to express her vision in ways that people "get it." Samantha has made that possible by helping me complete my children's books through using her considerable graphic and illustration talents.

Rachel Burse is a dedicated and exemplary model for corporate tenacity, patience, and excellence. Active is an understatement for this financial guru, wife, mother, community leader, and good friend. I appreciate her accomplishments, brilliance, and humanity coupled with humility.

Pamela L. Williams is an engineer. She has global responsibilities for a Fortune 50 (I believe it's ranked that high!) company, and she oversees the development of some of our most important and practical household products. She is gifted, caring, and a skilled manager of projects and of people. She's an avid art collector and she is a supportive and wonderful friend.

Tracy L. (Thomas) Prigmore is extremely bright, tenacious, and successful. She has been influencing me since I met her in college, and she showed me how great it feels to have fresh flowers daily. Between her real estate business, her medical administrative responsibilities, and being a loving, loyal, and productive wife and daughter, Tracy makes time for what's most important: relationships. She introduced me to business principles and shared the importance of having a plan and strategy for success. Though I still don't have an asset sheet for my personal worth, her contribution to my growth and development are invaluable.

The late Reverend Delores Francine McMillan helped me to get connected with my spiritual center by teaching and sharing the Bible. She extended her "works" by adopting me as her "God daughter," and by encouraging me to eat peppermint at times when patience was required, she helped me to learn how to listen enough to become successful.

I'm excited to Get Connected with you! For leadership or communication training or for presentations for you or to your group, connect with me at getconnected@absolutegood.com.

Quick Order Form

If you really liked this book, tell a friend, or buy a copy for them:

Buy "If You Really Want to Be Successful, Get Connected! TODAY!

Web: www.jolenajohnson.com
Email: books@absolutegood.com
We accept all major credit cards through PayPal:

c/o Absolute Good Training and Life Skills Management

Call or email today for checks, money orders, or
for quantity discounts. 240.644.2500

Name and Title _____

Organization _____

Address _____

City/State/Zip _____

Phone _____

E-mail _____

Please send me FREE Information on
☐ Books ☐ Speaking ☐ Training ☐ Seminar
☐ Good Projects Together

Please send me copies of "*If You Really Want to Be Successful, Get Connected!*" for $19.95 each plus $3.00 for shipping and handling. Please call for quantity discounts. Published by Mission Possible Press in conjunction with Absolute Good Training and Life Skills Management. THANK YOU!